CATALYST

THE SIMPLE SYSTEM TO ENERGIZE,
BUILD, AND SUSTAIN BUSINESS TEAMS
WHO KEEP ON WINNING

MICHAEL WOLSTEN

This book is dedicated to all the leaders who choose the road less traveled.

Contents

Is This Book For You?

Not sure if having a structured, scalable framework to move your team into greatness and giving your best to the world is really for you? Here are some burning doubts many have before they begin their journey toward leadership freedom:

"I won't have time to implement what's in this book."

I get it, you're busy running a team, juggling decisions, and keeping everything on track. *That's exactly why you need this book.* The ABC Framework streamlines your processes, gives you clear steps to follow, and, most importantly, frees up your time by making your team and systems run more efficiently. Think of it as investing in a system that'll save you time *as you grow.*

"I've tried frameworks and strategies before, what's different about this one?"

It's proven.

215 leadership teams from all across the country have implemented this and seen real growth, both in their people and their profits, within 90 days.

The ABC Framework is grounded in real-world experience, tested in companies like Starbucks and the nation's large credit unions, and has consistently delivered results.

This process is proven to lower turnover, increase productivity, measurably improve your culture, and equip your leadership team within the first 90 days.

"I don't think this applies to my business."

Think again. The ABC Framework isn't just for one specific type of business, it's built to help any organization, no matter the size or industry, build strong teams, enhance culture, and improve systems.

This book is for leaders who are responsible for guiding teams, creating momentum, and driving results, whether you're a senior executive, a credit union leader, or an entrepreneur building a high-performance culture.

It's helped for-profits, non-profits, family-owned businesses and mid-sized companies. I promise you: it has the power to transform your organization from the inside out.

"We've been doing fine without a structured framework, why change now?"

Let me ask you this: could things be going *even better*? Chances are you're missing something that would take your team to the next level.

A structured framework unlocks new levels of performance and consistency. Without a clear, repeatable system, you're relying on *luck* and *good in-*

tentions to keep things running smoothly. The most successful businesses optimize, adapt, and improve.

The ABC Framework helps you do exactly that, giving you a clear process for ongoing growth. The best leaders know that growing isn't optional and the next mountain is ready to be climbed. If this is you, I'd encourage you to keep reading.

STOP

Don't forget your bonuses!

4 powerful resources come with this book.

1. If you're a leader who has already built a measure of success, and you still have a deep internal drive to keep expanding, you've probably experienced the "leadership rollercoaster". Friday you feel on top of the world, and Tuesday you're overwhelmed.

What if you could eliminate the valleys and have consistent growth week after week? This Masterclass covers my **ABC Framework** in depth, the one many of my clients use to eliminate playing small, so they can pull off their leadership mission, critical priorities, and equip their team to do the same. This training contains some new material, not just a repeat of what I teach in this book.

2. Perhaps you're not sure how to discover your organization's true why? I'll give you my **Who Is Guide** for free. It'll get you and your team started in uncovering your Why, which will deepen your impact right away.

3. Information without action can leave you stuck. So, I created the **Leadership Snapshot**, a personalized assessment designed to help you diagnose your team's areas of strength and action steps to help you improve your results in less than 5 minutes.

4. Community and connection are key, so I'm giving you access to my weekly newsletter. Join like-minded leaders and learn lessons from the best organizations all across the country.

To get all 4 of these bonuses, just go here, stick in your name and email address, and you'll have them instantly!

https://michaelwolsten.com/catalyst-bonus

Introduction: Why the Old Way of Doing Leadership No Longer Sticks

Your team isn't the problem.

Not their talent, not their work ethic, not their commitment. But if you're like most leaders, there are days when it feels like something isn't clicking, when no matter how hard you push, your team isn't moving at the pace you need. The energy is off. The results aren't there. The momentum is slipping. And if you're honest, you're starting to wonder if you're the one holding them back.

I get it. I've been there. And I can tell you right now, you're not alone.

The Leadership Trap No One Talks About

Leading a team is about working smarter. And yet, most leaders are trapped in the same frustrating cycle. They start with vision, they get some early wins, and then, at some point, things slow down. Communication breaks down. Accountability slips. Meetings feel less productive. Performance plateaus.

And instead of diagnosing the real issue, what do most leaders do?

- They push harder.

- They take on more responsibility themselves

- They micromanage, or they step back too much, hoping the team will figure it out.

- They start questioning if they have the right people, or if they're cut out for this.

But what if the problem isn't you? And what if it's not your team either?

What if you're just approaching leadership the wrong way?

The ABC Framework helps you:

- Assess your team's real challenges, so you're solving the right problems.

- Build the structure, accountability, and communication needed for long-term success.

- Cultivate a culture of trust, ownership, and high performance, without burning yourself or your team out.

So that you and your team accomplish your vision and goals and perform at a high level.

Most leaders struggle because they rely on tactics without a strategy, one-off solutions that don't create real change. This book will help you understand why your team gets stuck, how to unlock their full potential, and what you need to do next.

Why This Matters (And Why I Wrote This Book)

I'm not writing this as a consultant looking in from the outside. I've lived this. I've led teams that struggled with accountability, communication, and execution. I've worked with leaders who were one bad quarter away from burnout. And I've seen firsthand what happens when a great leader finally gets the right tools to unlock their team's full potential.

Your team wants to perform at a high level. They want clarity. They want to feel ownership over their work. They want to trust their leader. But they can't do that unless you're leading in a way that creates that culture.

Don't Wait, Because Time Won't Wait for You

Here's the danger: most leaders know their team isn't operating at full capacity, and do nothing. They assume things will work themselves out. They wait for that "perfect hire" to come in and fix everything. They get caught up in the daily grind and never take the time to fix the root of the problem.

But ask yourself, how long has your team been running at less than full potential? Six months? A year? Longer?

That's lost revenue. Lost impact. Lost momentum.

And it won't fix itself.

This book isn't about "someday." It's about right now. The insights, frameworks, and strategies inside these pages are built for action. If you're ready to stop putting out fires, stop feeling like you have to carry the team on your back, and start leading in a way that actually works, let's go.

Because a high-performing team isn't something you stumble into. It's something you build.

Now, turn the page. Let's unlock it.

Two Types of Leaders:
Which One Are You?

I was five years old when my dad first taught me to build a fire. I grew up in the Pacific Northwest, where there always seemed to be four seasons of rain.

To handle these conditions and get a good fire going, he shared a few key things:

- You need dry wood. There's nothing worse than trying to start a fire with wood that has sat out in the rain for months.

- You need the right air flow. Even with the world's driest wood, improper spacing prevents fire from starting or makes it die quickly.

But the most important thing he shared?

You must have the right Catalyst.

Pine cones and needles, dryer lint, commercial fire starter, maybe even lighter fluid or gasoline (if you love losing your eyebrows or receiving calls from angry neighbors).

The Catalyst needs to be strong and provide lots of heat and be long lasting, so it can not only start the fire but help keep it going.

My two decades of coaching hundreds of leaders revealed that team leadership follows the same principles. The most effective leaders are **Catalysts**, the fire starters in their organization. They provide practical, daily actions that help their team live out their vision. They provide the consistent spark needed to help move projects, ideas, people and the mission of their organizations forward.

Often, these leaders don't realize how much of an impact they have on others. And when they do drift, it usually doesn't happen all at once. It happens after taking on a new role, picking up extra responsibilities without the right boundaries, or discovering that what got them here isn't working anymore.

That's when leaders can shift from being a **Catalyst** to a **Reactionist**.

Instead of helping their team keep their fire going, Reactionists are constantly putting out wildfires all around them.

Here are some key distinctions:

Reactionist: *Waits for issues to surface before taking action. They're constantly reacting, stuck in a loop of putting out fires.*

Catalyst: *Plans ahead. Anticipates friction. Puts systems in place before problems arise, minimizing chaos and maximizing impact.*

Reactionist: *Feels buried in the weeds. Every day is triage, handling what's urgent, instead of what's important.*

Catalyst: *Creates space to lead. Delegates. Empowers others. Makes time for strategy, culture, and coaching.*

Reactionist: *Avoids change or fears it. Clings to what worked before, even if it's no longer working.*

Catalyst: *Leans into change. Uses it as a tool for growth. Helps the team adapt, evolve, and come out stronger.*

Reactionist: *Leads from stress and frustration. That energy gets passed down, and the team feels it.*

Catalyst: *Leads with clarity, calm, and purpose. Their presence lifts the room, not drains it.*

Reactionist: *Solves in the moment. Focuses on the quick fix, often band-aiding deeper issues.*

Catalyst: *Thinks long-term. Builds systems that solve root problems and create momentum for the future.*

Reactionist: *Growth feels incremental. Dependent on external circumstances. Relies on familiar playbooks.*

Catalyst: *Growth becomes exponential. Aligned to a clear vision, consistent action, and cultural buy-in.*

Reactionist: *Feels the need to do it all. Struggles to turn it off. Delegation feels risky. Control feels safe.*

Catalyst: *Let's go of control to gain influence. Builds teams that lead alongside them, not beneath them.*

Reactionist: *Relies on authority to get alignment, especially under pressure. The message becomes "Do it because I said so."*

Catalyst: *Leads with collaboration. Gains buy-in. Builds shared ownership and pride in the process.*

Reactionist: *Plays it safe. Repeats what used to work. Sticks to the status quo, even when it's no longer delivering.*

Catalyst: *Encourages experimentation. Celebrates ideas. Pushes the team to challenge assumptions and think bigger.*

Reactionist: Burns out. Wears the weight of the world. Leaves behind a team that struggles to function without them.

Catalyst: Builds sustainable systems. Raises up leaders. Leaves behind a culture that continues to thrive, even when they step away.

What do you feel as you read through this list?

Do you feel some **Reactionist** descriptions landing more than the **Catalyst** ones?

If so, that's great news! There's nothing better than seeing the reality of your starting place so you can move forward with clarity.

As a leader, you decide which path to take.

Will you react and scramble?

Or will you lead with intention and become the Catalyst your team needs?

One leader I worked with, Angela, spent most of her time firefighting, handling daily crises, making reactive decisions, and feeling exhausted. After implementing the ABC Framework, she shifted her focus to long-term strategy, empowered her team, and freed herself from constant stress. The result?

She gained 10 hours back on her calendar, saw higher team engagement, improved clarity, and achieved consistent growth.

So how do you lead like a Catalyst?

You use a system designed to help you lead that way, consistently, practically, and sustainably.

That system is called the **ABC Framework**.

The ABC Leadership Framework
A Catalyst for Sustainable Growth

The strongest leaders, the ones who build teams that perform consistently and grow over time, follow a system.

That system is called the **ABC Framework: Assess, Build, Cultivate.**

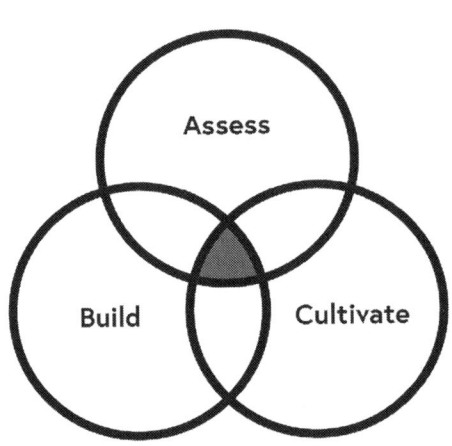

The ABC Framework is a simple, sustainable structure designed to help leaders:

- Gain clarity on what's really happening inside their team

- Build the systems that support long-term success

- Create the consistency needed to sustain performance over time

It works because it mirrors how successful leadership truly evolves, not through force or personality, but through intentional rhythm.

Let's take a closer look at each phase

Assess: Clarity Before Strategy

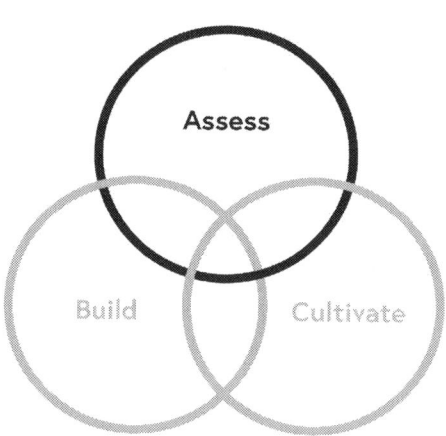

Before you can lead forward, you need to understand where you stand.

In the Assess phase, you focus on uncovering what's really happening within your team, your culture, and your leadership environment. What are people feeling but not saying? Where is there energy, or apathy? What's currently driving performance, and what might be holding it back?

This step starts with listening well, through surveys, conversations, and observation.

The most successful leaders lead from **Ground Truth.**

Build: Laying the Foundation for Sustainable Growth

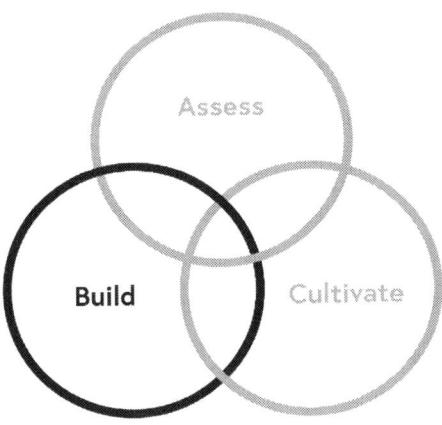

Once you know the truth, it's time to do something with it.

Build is where leadership becomes practical. In this phase, you create the scorecards, systems, structures, and development plans that support your vision and make growth possible.

A vision only becomes real when it's backed by structure.

Whether you're building a high-performance culture, launching a new initiative, or developing future leaders, this phase turns clarity into traction.

Cultivate: Sustaining Momentum with Consistency

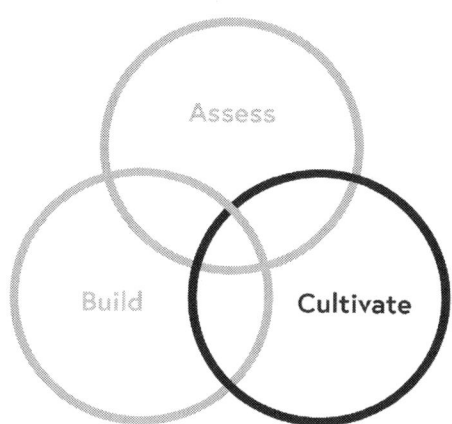

Growth that starts strong doesn't always last. That's where **Cultivate** comes in.

This is the rhythm of reinforcement. It's where leaders sustain momentum, strengthen engagement, and ensure that what gets built actually lasts.

This phase is about consistency.

You coach. You celebrate. You investigate when things drift. You realign your team around what matters most.

Why This Framework Works

The ABC Framework is a loop.

Each phase feeds into the next, and each time through the loop, your team becomes more aligned, more resilient, and more prepared for growth.

But what if you skip a step?

Here's what tends to happen when the system is incomplete:

- **Assess + Build, but no Cultivate** → You've built great systems, but they fade fast. Accountability slips. Staff engagement drops. It's like planting a garden and never watering it.

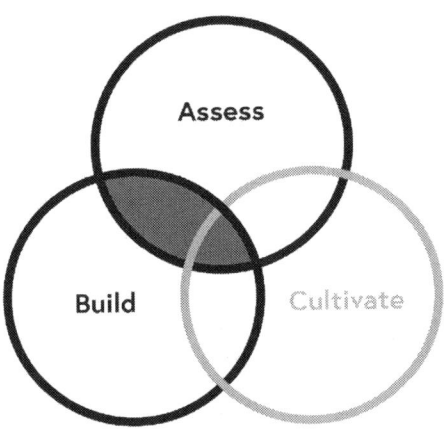

- **Build + Cultivate, but no Assess** → You're solving the wrong problems. Without ground truth, blind spots multiply. Turnover and misalignment catch you off guard.

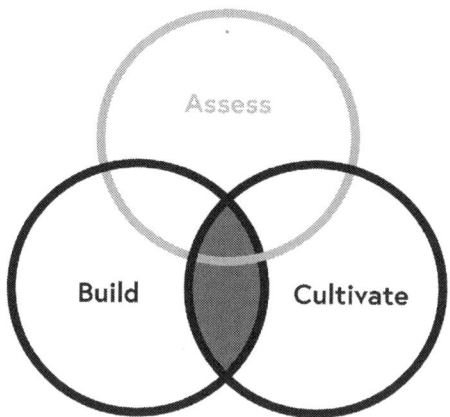

- **Assess + Cultivate, but no Build** → You've got awareness and reinforcement, but no clear direction. Morale might be high, but performance is inconsistent.

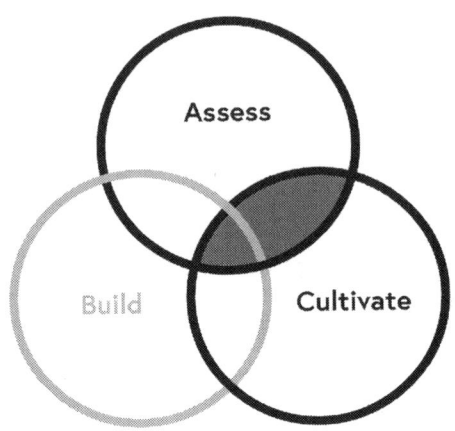

The Point? You Need All Three.

Great leaders don't just assess. They don't just build. They don't just cultivate. They do all three, in rhythm, in cycles, and with intention.

And that's what you're about to learn how to do.

In the next section, we'll dive into the first (and most foundational) phase: **Assess**.

You'll walk away with tools, stories, and strategies you can apply immediately to get your team aligned and moving forward.

Let's get to work.

PART ONE: ASSESS

TRUTH BEFORE STRATEGY

Chapter 1: Ground Truth
Why Leadership Starts With What's Actually Real

You can't fix what you can't see. Start by getting the truth on the table.

What kind of soil do you have?

Our goal in the Assess phase is to identify what I call the "Ground Truth", the reality of your team's internal operations. Consider the soil in a garden. When our family moved to Idaho, we had to figure out what our soil was like before we could plant anything.

The same is true in leadership, if you don't take time to understand your environment, your people, and your culture, you're planting seeds that may never take root.

I discovered that without the right soil mix, crops will struggle to grow, and your harvest may be little to none.

The best way to know what kind of soil you have is to get in there and till it. That means breaking it up to see what's underneath, which isn't an easy job. I remember when we built our garden. I spent hours on the tiller, walking behind it, picking out rocks, getting the pH tested, to see exactly what we had. Some areas were perfect for planting right away, while other sections needed a lot more work.

This experience reflects what happens in our teams and organizations. When we assess what's going on, there'll be areas that are rocky or hard to work with, just like tough soil. Sometimes, the tiller even bounces off the hard ground, or it's so packed that it's hard to move. The more we understand our Ground Truth, the better we can help our teams grow.

After having helped dozens of organizations till and test their soil, it's often arduous work and... it's vitally important. If we don't dig deep to understand what's under the surface, it'll be hard for things to grow the way we want them to.

As you go through this process, keep in mind that you might uncover things you don't like, rocky areas that are tough to work with. But you'll also find spots that are naturally good for growth.

This process naturally uncovers areas for you and your leadership team to grow in as well. All growth starts from the top down, so make sure you do everything possible to prepare your organization for true growth.

Chapter 2: Pulse Power
The Secret to Hearing What Your Team Isn't Saying

Most leaders sense these changes long before they can clearly define them. You might find yourself saying, "Something feels off, but I can't quite put my finger on it." That's because the signals are subtle. Until they're not.

The Ground Truth is what's actually happening: what your teams are experiencing and what's said "around the water cooler."

And the Ground Truth is always changing. Add in a new team member, have a toxic team member transfer departments, go through a particularly stressful or busy season, and the dynamics shift.

The Leadership Fog: "I Know Something's Off"

When clients share their concerns with me, there's often a sense that something is just a bit off. They say things like:

"Michael, I know things are good, but they're not great, and I don't know exactly how to get my team where we want to go."

"It feels like one or two pieces are off. I don't know how to get my team to tell me what they need to tell me so we can grow together."

One leader even confided:

"I know some really good people have left, and I can't pinpoint why. I might be part of the problem, or there might be a bigger piece of the story, but I just don't know what to do about it."

That's why the Assess phase is so important.

The more data you have, the more truth you can work with.

Why Measuring the Ground Truth Matters

Knowing where you are, and consistently measuring your team and culture, gives you:

- Actionable data you can use right away

- Consistent benchmarks to see progress quarter after quarter

- A proactive tool for feedback so you can spot trends before they become problems

Leaders are often so busy juggling daily demands that it feels almost impossible to slow down long enough to ask where everyone really is. But in reality, this slow-down is what makes your speed sustainable.

In fact, some of the highest-performing teams consider this process the most important ingredient to their success. One credit union client shared:

"We know we can keep driving forward, but we didn't know the tweaks needed to stay on the road and make the ride faster and smoother."

Your Team is Too Nice to Tell You the Truth

Even though most leaders want open feedback, they often don't know how to ask the right questions or create the right environment to get real answers.

Some team members avoid sharing anything that might "rock the boat." Others don't know how to express their concerns in a way that feels safe or productive. On the flip side, some might be overly blunt or frustrated, and their feedback can be hard to receive.

That's where Pulse Surveys come in.

Assess: Pulse Surveys

Pulse Surveys are the most effective way to gather valuable feedback. When you ask the right questions, at the right frequency, in the right way... you get incredible data that helps you know the Ground Truth.

So, how does it work? There are a few key elements:

- The survey needs to be **short**, **targeted**, and **anonymous**.

- I recommend around 20 questions that cover key areas such as:

  ○ How satisfied are you with the work you're doing?

  ○ Do you feel valued in your work?

  ○ Do you have clarity in your role and goals?

If you're not sure which questions to ask or how to best collect this data, head over to https://michaelwolsten.com and send me a message to see if you qualify for a **free Pulse Survey** for your organization.

Once you have data from these surveys, you can benchmark where your team is as you make organizational changes. This makes it easier to see what's working, and where to focus next.

Gallup, in their *State of the Global Workplace Report* (2021), found that when teams regularly get feedback and feel their voices are heard, their productivity goes up by almost **15%**. Employees asked for input are also more engaged, with **59% reporting higher engagement** compared to just **36%** for those not regularly surveyed.

A Personal Story: When I Got It Wrong

One story that highlights the need for knowing the Ground Truth comes from my own leadership journey.

When I first started as a leader, I thought I had it all figured out. (I was in my early 20s.)

But I didn't have a solid grasp on my team, what motivated them, or how to lead them as individuals. And I wasn't open to feedback.

Why?

Because I was too focused on "faking it until I made it." And that advice nearly ruined my team.

In just one month, I lost **four out of seven** team members. Most of them gave generic, surface-level reasons for leaving:

"It's crazy, I wasn't even looking, but then someone reached out."

It never sat right with me. So I asked one team member directly:

"What's the real reason you're leaving, even if it's something I don't want to hear?"

She paused. Then she said something I'll never forget:

"I feel that you like us, but you don't really care about what we think or do. You like us as people, but it's hard to see how you care about us individually."

That hit hard. I realized I wasn't asking the right questions, and I wasn't creating a safe enough space for people to speak up.

That conversation became a turning point in how I led moving forward.

You can't lead well if you're only guessing at what your team needs. Pulse surveys reveal what's true. But truth is just the beginning.

Now that you've surfaced where things really stand, the next step is just as important:

Assess: Quarterly Action Plans

After gathering data from your Pulse Surveys, the next step is to create action plans with your team on a quarterly basis.

It's critical to share these action steps with your team, based on their feedback, to help close the loop and show them you're serious about tackling these areas together.

Pulse surveys cover a lot of ground and help you see what frameworks need to be deployed first. Sometimes One-on-Ones are inconsistent. Development Plans are outdated. Coaching isn't happening regularly. But now, you have a roadmap.

One client discovered through the survey that their one-on-ones and team meetings weren't as effective as they thought. There were many distractions, and the meetings felt haphazard.

So the leader made a commitment to improve the quality of meetings, including frequency and focus. The team member committed to showing up prepared. Together, they redefined their rhythm.

In this phase, remember: **responsibility isn't solely on the leader or the team member**. You must come together, understand the feedback, and build solutions collaboratively.

Assess: Client Results

Tracking progress over time is like taking soil samples to monitor the health of your garden. As you till the soil to see what's underneath, you gain the clarity needed to make smart changes.

One of my clients went through this process after losing a few "bad apples." The remaining team members were strong, culture-oriented individuals. But when we went through the Pulse Survey, she identified hidden issues.

Even though the team was full of great people, they were struggling with being direct with one another, and had no idea how to handle difficult conversations.

If she had assumed everything was fine, she would have missed a huge opportunity for growth. But because she committed to discovering the Ground Truth and running Pulse Surveys, she could identify the real issue and address it. And her team got better.

Another client saw a **22% increase in engagement** over 9 months after implementing changes based on their Pulse Survey results and action plans. Their leadership team stabilized after some transitions the year before, and the organization experienced **39% year-over-year growth**.

These results weren't random. They happened because the leader made space for truth, action, and consistent reassessment.

Chapter 3: Talent Radar
Spotting Strengths, Gaps, and Hidden Stars

Once we've gained a better understanding of the "soil" we're working with, it's time to dig deeper into the strengths of our team, to see how everyone fits together for maximum effectiveness.

Why start here?

Because if we don't identify what's working, we risk dismantling the very things that are holding our teams together.

Strengths First: Rethinking the Well-Rounded Myth

Let me give you an example from early in my leadership journey that changed how I approach this entire process...

When it comes to strengths-based management, there's a myth that we must be a "jack of all trades..."

I remember asking my high school teacher why we needed to learn Precalculus equations and how it would help me in the real world. "To help you become more well-rounded," he responded. Even back then, something felt a bit off about the whole thing.

It wasn't until I got into college and picked my own leadership classes that I fully understood the problem. By focusing on being well-rounded, I didn't allow myself the time to focus on really diving into my strengths and giftings.

We're often told to focus on our weaknesses and work on improving them to ensure we can at least "get by" in major areas. This philosophy aims for everyone to have at least a basic understanding of subjects. However, the full quote from earlier is: **"Jack of all trades, master of none."**

That day, I realized something: If you don't define your strengths clearly, you'll never know what you are truly great at and what you can fully master.

This is why I love focusing on **Strengths-Based Coaching**. It's often a completely different approach than many of us grew up with. It emphasizes identifying and enhancing our strengths first, which can help us become a lot more productive and effective.

Target Practice: A Strengths-Based Illustration

Let's imagine you asked me to take a bucket of 50 baseballs and throw them from second base to home plate. Someone is standing as the catcher.

Now, I'm not a great athlete (not Charlie Brown bad, either), but if I were to throw these baseballs with my right arm, I'd get them fairly close to home plate every time. Because I'm right-handed, I'd do a decent job.

The same exercise with my left arm would be a completely different experience. The throws would be erratic, uncomfortable, and much less accurate.

This scenario mirrors what I see in leadership. Often, we don't take the time to ask ourselves, *"What am I naturally gifted at?"* or *"What are my strengths as a leader?"* Instead of focusing on improving areas where we're not as strong, we could be asking how to lean into our natural talents.

Even worse, we don't do that with our team... and then get frustrated when they're pitching left-handed.

Why Strengths Work: The Research

Utilizing this approach in a structured way can result in some big payoffs for your organization:

- **Performance:** Strengths-based approaches led to a 14% improvement in job performance across the sample compared to those focused on weaknesses or traditional management approaches. *(The Power of Strengths-Based Development: A Meta-Analysis, 2020)*

- **Employee Engagement:** There was a 20% increase in employee engagement in organizations using strengths-based leadership compared to those using traditional leadership models. *(Strengths-Based Leadership: An Exploration of Effectiveness, 2021)*

- **Retention:** Organizations that implemented strengths-based approaches saw a 15% decrease in turnover rates compared to those relying on more conventional management styles. *(A Strengths-Based Approach to Employee Motivation and Well-Being, 2022)*

How Teams Leverage Strengths-Based Tools

Gallup and other organizations have gathered a lot of information on this topic. In my experience with clients, we see great results after strength assessments.

There's often a 29% increase in overall team satisfaction within the first 6 months of leveraging some key Strengths-Based coaching frameworks. By identifying and articulating strengths, teams can operate much more cohesively and leverage their superpowers in new ways.

Once we know a team member's specific strength, I can talk about their unique abilities, whether it's their strength in activating action, their ability to form deeper connections, or their relationship-building skills. This gives us a common language to better collaborate.

Finding Your Fit Partner

I can also identify what I call a "fit partner." If I'm weak in an area, I can pinpoint someone on the team who's naturally strong in that area. This helps us work together more effectively, creating a more balanced team environment.

I once worked closely with a colleague who had complementary strengths. I love speaking to people, presenting on stage, and leading from the front. She, on the other hand, loved being behind the scenes. She excelled at analyzing data, diving into spreadsheets, and understanding why things were happening, or not happening. Although I can do that, it's not where my natural strength lies.

So we leveraged each other's strengths. I'd handle the front-facing tasks, and she'd take charge of the data and analysis. We weren't using or manipulating each other; instead, we worked together to complement each other's natural strengths. We actually amplified them by focusing more on our skills and interests.

Open communication about our strengths improved our effectiveness and efficiency. The results were clear: We experienced significant growth and our projects achieved better outcomes by becoming a dynamic duo.

Team Mapping and Alignment

Examples like this are why I love **Team Mapping**, which helps you see the best in your organization. It allows you to identify where individuals align well together, where they might need additional support, and where there are gaps in your team.

As your organization grows or as you add new team members, team mapping helps you determine what strengths are needed for new roles, ensuring that your team remains balanced.

One client brought me in to help do this with his team. Their team was very service-driven. Once we deployed the assessments and team mapping, a surprising development happened.

We had a team of mostly incredibly positive people, but none of them knew how to communicate expectations and experiences with team members that weren't the "glass half full" type. This meant strong team members, who were vital to the team's success and brought an important critical counterbalance, were leaving. Because they were in the dark half the time!

So we went through all their strengths and highlighted some frameworks that helped them to be bolder in addressing issues as they came up, especially with people who didn't have the "positive" strength. This allowed them to become far more transparent and proactive, and they're already seeing a boost in overall engagement in just a few weeks.

Another client used team mapping to help them find their next great hire. We went through what she really needed in the position, what her team makeup was, and determined that she needed someone with more strategic thinking and executing strengths to help balance out their relationship-driven team.

Mapping allows us to see how to leverage each team's unique make-up and overcome any barriers or issues through the lens of their strengths. Not only is this approach much more effective than just telling teams to "try harder" in a certain area, it gives each person ownership to lean more into what they're already great at.

Strengths in Action

Let's say you have a team member who excels in strategic thinking but struggles with detailed execution.

By reviewing their strengths quarterly, you can continue to fine-tune their development plan to ensure they're being assigned tasks that play to their strengths, (strategic planning, creative problem-solving, and big-picture thinking) while delegating or partnering them with someone who excels in execution. This not only increases productivity but also creates a more cohesive, high-functioning team.

Strength assessments aren't just a one-time exercise to check off your to-do list. It's crucial to include them as part of an ongoing process, and review them at least every 3 months to ensure that your team members are aligned with their strengths and continuously developing.

Why Strengths Lead to Growth

People grow exponentially when they work within their areas of strength. Gallup research shows that employees who use their strengths every day are **6 times more likely to be engaged** in their work and **3 times more likely to report having an excellent quality of life.**

This simple act, sharing what was already working, gave the team a tool they didn't even know they needed.

Before You Turn the Page...

Take 3 minutes to list your team's current bright spots.

What's working within your team's strengths that you don't want to lose?

Chapter 4: The 3 C's
The Secret to Building a Team You Can Trust

Once you've identified what's working, the next question becomes: Who on your team can carry that momentum forward, and how do you know?

Years ago, when I was opening credit union branches all across Idaho, I needed a repeatable way to identify the right people, those who would thrive in new environments, new cities, and new markets.

I could assess their strengths and experience, but I didn't have a reliable filter to know whether they'd be top performers. That's when I began developing a practical framework I now call the "3 C's."

This simple but powerful tool helped me identify whether someone had the foundation to grow with the team and contribute at a high level. Over time, I discovered that the best team members, I could build around, were consistently high in 3 areas:

Committed, Capable, and Coachable.

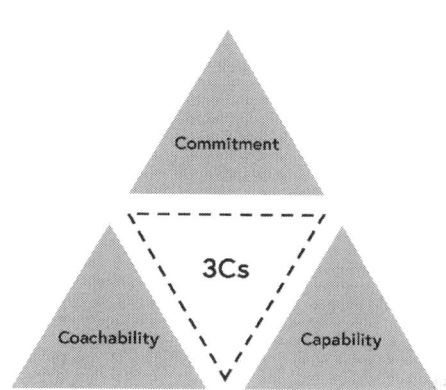

These 3 qualities showed up in every top performer I worked with. And just as importantly, when any of these traits were lacking, performance suffered. Misalignment in the 3 C's leads to inconsistency, frustration, and limited growth. Not just for the individual, but for the whole team.

Let's break each one down.

Committed

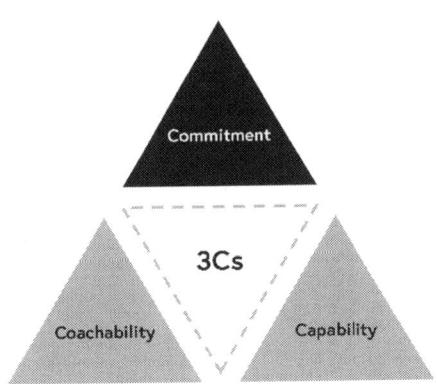

Commitment is about dedication to the mission, consistency in the work, and showing up with energy even when it's hard. A committed team member does the right thing, even when no one is watching.

To assess commitment, I often ask:

- Do they follow through on what they say they'll do?

- Do they give their best, even when it's inconvenient?

- Are they fully engaged in the mission and culture?

When someone is rated a 7 in commitment, dig into the "why."

What are their strengths in this area? Where do they need clarity or support?

Great coaching always starts with asking better questions, so you can get better context.

Capable

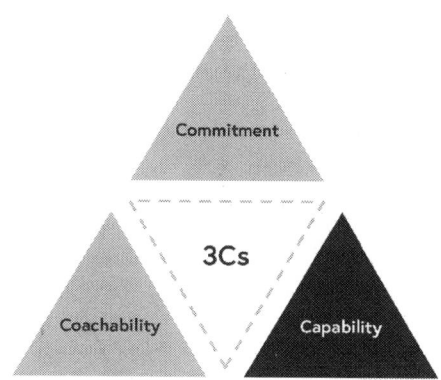

Capability isn't about being perfect in a role. It's about the capacity to grow into it. A capable team member shows potential. They're able to learn, improve, and adapt.

Ask yourself:

- Have they demonstrated the ability to grow in the past 6–12 months?

- Do they take initiative?

- Can they stretch into bigger responsibilities?

A newer employee may not have everything figured out yet, but if they're taking feedback, learning quickly, and solving problems, they're showing capability.

Coachable

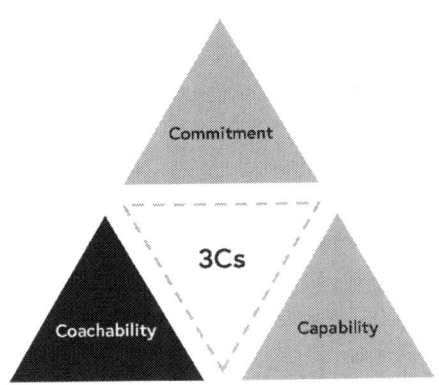

Of the 3, coachability is often the hardest to assess, but it's the one that unlocks real transformation. Coachable people are open to feedback. They listen. They evolve.

Someone can be incredibly talented but stall out if they resist coaching. I've worked with high performers who relied too much on their natural strengths and stopped growing the moment things got tough.

Look for patterns:

- Do they respond with curiosity or defensiveness?

- Are they applying feedback, or just nodding in meetings?

- Are they evolving in how they show up?

Coachability isn't about being passive, it's about being willing. Willing to stretch, learn, and let someone else guide you through discomfort.

How to Use the 3 C's to Coach Your Team

After evaluating each person across the 3 C's (on a 1–10 scale), you can begin having focused, strategic coaching conversations. The goal isn't to label anyone, it's to identify where growth is possible.

A few coaching tips:

- **Use permission-based language.** Ask, "Are you open to some feedback that could help you grow in this area?"

- **Give examples.** Be clear and specific. Vague feedback won't help someone improve.

- **Co-create a plan.** Growth needs accountability. You bring the direction; they bring the effort.

A collaborative development plan should include:

1. Specific areas for growth with actions and timelines

2. What the team member is committing to

3. What you're committing to as their leader

And here's the kicker: this isn't just for them. It's also for you.

The 3 C's as a Mirror for Leadership

How are you doing in these areas?

- **Committed:** Are you still showing up with energy and purpose?

- **Capable:** Are you growing as a leader, or coasting on what you've always done?

- **Coachable:** Are you open to feedback, or operating like you already know the answer?

The 3 C's are both a filter for evaluating others, and a reflection of our own leadership. If you model these traits, your team will follow.

Take five minutes and look at your direct reports.

Who has all 3? Who's missing one, and how's it impacting the team?

Once you've identified the players you can build around, it's time to talk about what to do next with that information.

Chapter 5: Destroying Roadblocks
What to Do With All This Data

Your next step is to build rhythm into how you use that data. That means revisiting these insights quarterly, not just when someone's performance starts slipping. Pulse checks. Scorecard reviews. Culture and engagement surveys. These are your early detection tools.

But there's more.

Beyond individual evaluations, we need to look at team dynamics. This is where team mapping becomes critical.

* Who works best with whom?

* Where are the communication gaps?

* How do individual strengths complement, or conflict with, each other?

By mapping out how each person fits into the team, you can build better partnerships, align responsibilities, and create synergy. The best teams don't just have talent, they have alignment.

Use the 3 C's to assess your team at every level:

* Individually

- Within departments

- Across leadership

And of course, don't forget to apply this lens to yourself and your leadership team.

The best leaders I know aren't just assessing others, they're constantly assessing themselves. They're asking:

- What strengths do I bring right now?

- Where am I the bottleneck?

- Am I truly modeling what I expect from my team?

That's what sets high-growth organizations apart. They don't just gather data. They do something with it.

How to Not Get in Your Own Way

Here's a collection of things that I often hear when we start implementing these frameworks and the challenges that leaders face. Maybe you can relate with some of them.

You might be thinking, "This all sounds great, Michael, but how am I going to get my team on board? Some people on my team won't handle these conversations well." It's a valid concern.

The assessment phase isn't just about assessing your team, it's about assessing your own approach as a leader. Every leader is in a growth process and has the ability to make course corrections.

You can step back and say, "Here's what I've done well, and here's what I want to improve." When you give yourself grace, you'll be able to extend that grace to your team and have more credibility in helping them move forward.

I also get that there might be specific barriers. Perhaps it's a conversation you're avoiding with someone, or you're unsure how to handle certain issues.

I had one client once tell me,

"I think the reason I've put off talking to my team about this is because I feel hypocritical. I struggle with being accurate and yet I'm trying to coach and correct them to do something I'm not doing? It just feels off..."

In the situation above, I helped the leader see that because he struggled with the same thing, he actually had more power to address it.

I said,

"What do you think it could look like if you were 100% transparent with your team? What if you addressed the issue head on?

You could say, "Team, I've been struggling with how to address accuracy within our team because in part, I struggle with it too. So, I let things slide and then everyone, including our customers, feel the fallout. I'm committed to doing things differently from here on out and need us to all improve our accuracy, starting with me. This means I'm going to ask for your help when you see issues pop up and I'm going to hold everyone to a higher standard, starting today. Our customers and our team deserve it. Are you all committed to helping us improve and receive feedback as we move forward?"

After this conversation and spending a few weeks focusing on accuracy (how to fix errors before they start, holding each other accountable, tracking success/error free days), the entire team went from one of the worst in accuracy to the best location in the company within 60 days...

That's the power of asking the right questions, getting the right data, and acting on it to help you and your team make real change happen incredibly fast.

Perhaps you're concerned about how you or others may feel when you address the opportunity areas that come up from the assessment phase. Is your hesitation about hurting someone's feelings or about avoiding a negative reaction? Have you been avoiding hard conversations because you're scared they'll go sideways, or you'd rather avoid the discomfort?

The key here is honesty and integrity, not just with your team but with yourself. Listen to what you're saying and, more importantly, listen to what you're not saying. It's important to lean into those hard conversations. When you approach them with care, integrity, and heart, positive change follows.

When this happens, here are questions to ask yourself:

What needs to be said to help this person move forward?

Even though it might be uncomfortable for them or me, what needs to be communicated and acted on for their benefit and growth?

When we stop to focus on these types of questions, we pull ourselves out of the emotion and look at the big picture.

Another way to get in your own way during the Assess phase is through frustration. A client once said to me, "I don't get it. I've done everything for them, bonuses, extra perks, all kinds of benefits. It's like they don't even care what I do."

Feeling unappreciated for your hard work is disheartening, but don't let frustration cloud your judgment.

Instead, focus on the data objectively. What are the actionable steps you can take, even if they seem small? You can't solve everything right away, but you can identify the low-hanging fruit and make progress.

Don't let negativity or self-pity stop you from moving forward. Embrace the feedback, take action, and you'll strengthen yourself, your leaders, and your entire team, all at the same time.

Permission-Based Coaching

With permission-based coaching, you focus on getting buy-in throughout the process, which works wonders for navigating tough conversations. You explain the *why* behind what you're doing and ensure that everyone understands how it benefits not only them but the entire organization.

I once helped a leader who needed to have a tough conversation with one of their team members about their coachability. Instead of the usual "compliment sandwich" approach, the leader took a direct route. She explained the why before addressing the issue, saying something like:

"Josh, I wanted to give you some feedback, based on some things I have been seeing. Is now a good time to talk?"

By starting with the why, the leader created a more open, honest conversation. This allowed her to move beyond surface-level pleasantries and dive straight into the core issue.

It also allows the team member to tell you if they're ready to talk about the issue you want to share. The answer might be, "Not right now." They may not be in a great place to talk, may be in the middle of a bigger project or issue, or may want some time to think and prepare for the conversation.

Here's where permission-based coaching comes in: The leader asked if it was an okay time to talk and proceeded with clarity. She was real, transparent, and created space for the person to agree to the conversation.

Sometimes, leaders avoid tough conversations because they feel guilty or hypocritical. Perhaps they haven't been consistent with their own behaviors. With permission-based coaching, it's okay to acknowledge those struggles. Let the person know it's not about being perfect, it's about addressing areas that need growth.

Once the issue is laid out, the next step is to get commitments. This could be about what both the leader and the team member are willing to do moving forward. You can ask, "What are you willing to commit to in order to improve?" By phrasing it this way, you build trust and accountability.

Bringing It All Together

The Assess phase is about doing the hard work upfront:

- Understanding your team's soil

- Making the necessary changes

- Consistently tracking progress over time

By doing this, you create better soil, which establishes better roots, and sets the stage for consistent, healthy growth.

PART TWO: BUILD

INSTALLING THE FOUNDATION FOR
GROWTH THAT LASTS

Chapter 6: The Big 5

What Every High-Performing Team Must Get Right

Once you know where you stand, it's time to build what your team needs to thrive.

I've helped create this **Build phase** and have deployed it with multiple companies, which has proved to be a powerful framework.

These 5 areas are sequential. Each one builds on the last and must be approached in the right order:

1. Culture

2. Service

3. Growth

4. Finances

5. Systems

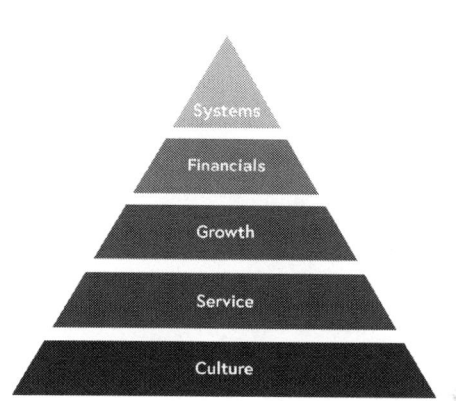

Jumping ahead or focusing on the later phases will minimize the effectiveness of your plan and, unfortunately, will end up looking like most other business plans.

The Big 5

The 5 categories encompass the specific areas of focus as you build your business. They provide a roadmap for creating your strategic plans, succession plans, and everything in between.

These elements feed into one another and are interconnected. By working on one, you support and amplify the others. Let's break down these areas and how they contribute to your success.

Culture: The Soil That Everything Grows From

Culture is the soil of your organization. If it's dry, rocky, or neglected, nothing else will grow, no matter how much strategy you layer on top.

In the Assess phase we talked about people and culture, evaluating the human assets within your organization. As a culture strategist, I've helped teams strengthen their culture for decades, and I believe there's no more powerful growth engine than having a healthy team culture.

No matter how many systems or finances you have, it's hard to create the momentum that leads to real growth without a solid culture in place.

Culture always comes first. Without the right culture, your company will always struggle to scale or perform to its potential.

Many companies mistakenly focus first on areas like finances and systems, the tech stack, the CRMs, etc. Although these are important, they're secondary to building the right environment and having the right people running your organization.

Because culture is the soil, it must be fertile before planting any seeds of growth. Cultivate that soil, dig deeper, and start with the people who'll ultimately drive the success of your business.

One question I sometimes get is, "Can you spend too much time focusing on your culture and people?"

The short answer is *yes*. It's possible, but not likely.

Why? Because with all the responsibilities leaders carry, it's usually very difficult for leaders to make consistent, meaningful time to connect with their team, even if they're trying to! It's not natural or easy for most leaders.

The leaders who ask me this question are often operating from a limited or outdated view of what it means to invest in culture and people. They often point to more parties, team gatherings, benefits, or hanging out. While none of these are wrong to do, building a strong culture focuses on a completely different framework and paradigm, as we'll uncover in the next chapter.

My approach focuses on what team members really want: to be valued and find deep satisfaction in the work they do. You can't over-invest in that, because the more you invest, the more the ROI will grow.

Service: Providing Value Through the Right People

Once you've built trust internally, your team becomes capable of creating trust externally.

At this point, we have the ability to provide excellent customer service because we've built a strong foundation of the right people (in the Assess stage) and culture. It's impossible to provide exceptional service when a great Culture and Service aren't in place. How do I know?

I'm sure you've been to businesses and felt the atmosphere the moment you walked in. I remember walking into an empty restaurant where the staff wasn't even talking to one another. It felt like a ghost town: no energy, no spark. A waiter saw me and looked at his coworker like, 'Oh, great. Now we have to help someone...' I immediately turned around and left.

On the other hand, I frequently visit a coffee shop with a "neighborhood bar" vibe. The baristas know me by name, remember my drink, and even joke about my changes in orders (I've committed to going decaf only, but some days I just need a little half caf boost). I enjoy spending my time and money there because of the energy, the connection, and the vibe.

With the right people and the right culture in place, your service quality will improve, which creates a deeper connection with your customers. This connection drives business. Service doesn't just happen by chance. I'm going to show you how you can build an award winning, service first organization, because it's built on proven frameworks that hundreds of leaders have used to help them win.

Growth: The Natural Outcome of Culture and Service

Growth is what happens when culture and service align, and when your people are fully engaged in the mission.

I've witnessed, over and over again, how a strong culture and top-tier service enables businesses to grow consistently, sustainably, and even exponentially.

Without these foundational elements, growth can be erratic, filled with spikes and drops, and inconsistencies that stunt the long-term success of your business. But when you have the right frameworks in place, growth becomes inevitable.

Finances: The Outcome of a Strong Foundation

Never start with finances. They're the natural result of what you're doing every day to serve your customers, grow your business, and foster a healthy work environment.

No one gets excited about finances outside of your accounting team, the CFO, some of your executives, and perhaps your board (if you have one). This is where the disconnect can start for many businesses.

The leadership team has financial outcomes, incentives, focus areas and because of their outlook, they expect everyone in the organization to understand and get behind net income growth or an uptick in profitability from last quarter...but what excites people are the things that drive the numbers: culture, service, and growth. By focusing on these elements, the money flows in naturally.

To sustain this momentum, it's critical to align financial goals with the daily actions of your team. This means translating high-level metrics like revenue or profit margins into tangible behaviors that everyone can rally behind.

For example, a team that prioritizes exceptional service naturally drives customer retention, which boosts recurring revenue. By fostering a culture where employees feel empowered to innovate and solve problems, you create efficiencies that reduce costs and improve margins.

When your people understand how their work connects to the bigger financial picture—without being bogged down by spreadsheets—they're more motivated to contribute to the organization's success.

We'll dive more into the how in the Finances chapter.

Systems: Supporting Growth and Scale

Once you have your people, culture, growth, and finances in place, then you're ready to invest in systems, like CRMs, productivity tools, and other technology that will support your business as it scales.

Systems come last. They should be in place to support your growth, not drive it.

I had a client fall into the trap of believing that changing a system would cure all their issues. She runs a credit union where the core processor was being changed out. (This is basically the main way to conduct transactions and the driver for all their other systems.)

It takes years of planning, late nights, and all hands-on deck to switch core processors. She commented,

"Once we get this new core system, it'll be so much easier and our teams will feel more comfortable talking to our members about new products and services and help us grow."

The truth is people don't change their approach to service and selling unless they discover what barriers are in place for them internally, learn a new way, and have accountability tools to embrace that new approach.

A new system to take in deposits won't change any of that.

It's a common myth that a new technology will change how people lead, serve, or sell. The truth is technology can help support behavior, but it doesn't shape it.

Remember, technology and systems evolve over time. When new tools come out, you'll need to adjust, anyway. That's why systems are a supporting player, not the main character. By focusing on the people, culture, and growth, you'll be able to adapt and scale your systems as needed, as well as handle any new disruptor or technology shift with ease.

As we explore each of these five phases, keep one thing in mind: You're building the conditions for people to thrive.

Chapter 7: Culture by Design
Building the Environment You and Your A-Players Love

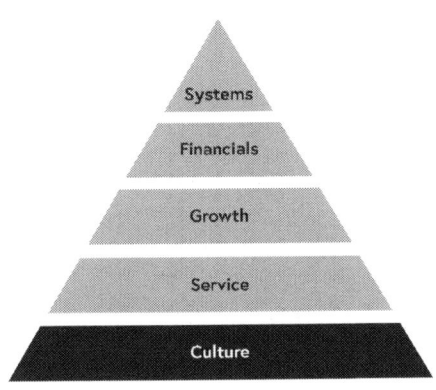

Culture is what you actively shape. Now that you've uncovered where your team stands, this next phase is about building the culture you want, with practical tools that reinforce your values every day.

We've already touched on this in the pulse survey, asking questions about what your team is feeling, but now I want to give you some additional tools that can help you shape your culture.

Regrounding Your Team: Identity Before Strategy

Before chasing new goals or launching your next strategic plan, take a moment to ask a more foundational question:

Who are we?

It's a question many teams skip, but without clarity on purpose and identity, even the best strategies fall flat. I've seen it across roles and industries: when people lose touch with why they're doing the work, momentum fades.

That's why I encourage teams to pause at least once a year for the **"Who Is" Exercise**. It's a simple but powerful way to help everyone, from frontline to leadership, realign with their purpose and who they serve.

Because when identity is clear, execution gets easier. Let's walk through how a few key questions can unlock clarity, connection, and performance.

'Who is' Exercise

This exercise helps everyone in your organization understand their roles and identities through key questions.

I often see a misalignment of understanding within the team about why they do what they do and who they represent. This includes frontline staff, volunteers, board members, and even leadership.

Running this exercise annually can help realign your team's identity and their purpose, which is vital when transitioning into a new strategic plan or setting new goals. When your team is aligned with these core principles, they'll hit the ground running.

Below are a few key questions to get you started:

- Why are you here? (what drives you personally?)

- Who do you serve?

- Is there anything holding you back?

- What do you want to be known for?

These questions may seem simple, but they unlock real outcomes. Consider the following research:

- Performance: Those who felt their work was meaningful performed 25% better on key performance metrics compared to employees who didn't perceive their work as meaningful. (The Impact of Meaningful Work on Employee Engagement: A Study of the Role of Purpose, 2020)

- Organizational Commitment: Those who found meaning in their daily tasks had 18% higher organizational commitment, leading to lower turnover rates. (The Role of Meaning and Purpose in Employee Well-being and Organizational Commitment, 2021)

- Team Collaboration: Teams where members felt their work contributed to a greater purpose showed 19% higher levels of collaboration and team cohesion compared to those without this sense of purpose. (Purpose and Job Performance: The Critical Role of Meaning in the Workplace, 2022)

We often dive into the How and What in business, but don't slow down often enough for the Why. Going through questions like these regularly, and framing our work through these lenses, can be incredibly powerful in our daily work.

With these types of results, how can we not slow down, just for a few minutes to ask and reaffirm some of these questions, so that teams can share the deeper why behind their work?

Two Rules That Shape a Healthy Team Culture

When it comes to building a strong, consistent team, what you tolerate matters just as much as what you teach.

In this section, we'll explore two practical culture-shaping tools: **The 24-Hour Rule** and **Honor the Absent**. Both help create an environment where trust grows, conflict gets addressed in a healthy way, and your team learns how to communicate with clarity and respect.

These aren't just ideas, they're guiding principles. When your team lives by them, the difference is obvious. Let's take a closer look.

The 24-Hour Rule

This is for managing conflict and difficult conversations.

If you experience an issue, particularly one that's emotional or difficult, address it within 24 hours, but not when you're emotionally charged.

This gives you time to step back, think it through, and take the emotion out of your response.

I've struggled with this as a leader. Once, a fellow executive sent an email to a group, explaining what couldn't be done and how my request wasn't helpful (in front of the rest of the group). After I got done reading it, I remember thinking, "Who does he think he is? Doesn't he realize he's calling me out in front of everyone, saying it can't be done and offering zero solutions?" And so, full of frustration (and what I thought was a measured, professional response), I sent a reply email. To this day, I don't remember my exact response, or the arguments I tried to articulate. But I remember exactly how I felt writing that email. My whole negative tone, my emotions, and my frustration came through loud and clear.

The moment I hit send, *I regretted it immediately.*

I knew there had to be a better way to communicate with this leader, instead of my passive aggressive email response. After about 30 minutes of thinking about it and calming down a bit, I picked up the phone to talk to this leader directly. I apologized for my response and explained how I felt about the situation.

In less than 5 minutes we came up with a solution (and the leader apologized for their approach during the call, too).

So what's the lesson here? When you delay the immediate response, you give yourself the chance to process things and approach the issue with a clearer mind. You'll avoid saying something rash or unproductive.

In my case, 30 minutes of waiting and processing would've made a world of difference.

By still focusing on the timeliness (addressing it within 24 hours) instead of bringing up issues from weeks ago, you address them quickly, so behaviors can be acknowledged and corrected. And by waiting until you cool off, you can help ensure your responses are more balanced and effective.

This rule can be applied not just as a leader, but across the whole team, helping prevent miscommunications and improving overall conflict resolution. It helps your organization be proactive and move past potential roadblocks faster.

Honor the Absent

Culture is also shaped by what we say when people aren't listening.

The rule is: Don't talk about people differently when they aren't in the room. Even well-intentioned conversations can turn unproductive and into vent sessions, saying things we would never say if they were present.

A client of mine had a lot of gossip going on in the organization. Many of them saw it as harmless or just a way to blow off some steam. So I asked this group of leaders a few questions.

"How does it change things if you're the one being talked about by others in a negative light?"

"Do you ever want to get out of conversations where someone 'just needs to vent for a bit' because you know there won't be any resolution from it?"

"Are the conversations you're having, without that person or group in the room, the same conversations you'd be having if they were present?"

Once we see the impact of our conversations, the damage caused by entertaining conversations like this, it can prompt us to change it. After some dialogue back and forth through our leadership training, the CEO said,

"Michael, I can see how we've all participated in this. The big question is, how do we correct it?"

I loved the ownership and desire for change that this leader expressed. Here's what I shared with them, to help them build a culture of trust and start honoring the absent:

- Make things right and commit to a new way. The most powerful and effective way to start this change is to have it come from the top down. When your leadership team decides that you'll Honor the Absent in all your conversations, some will course correct right away. You'll notice how you and others talk differently about customers, board members, volunteers, community members, politicians and, well, everyone.

- Help teams know what to do. This may include giving them new phrases to say, such as, "Hey, let's talk about something else. I don't want to talk about x without them being here." Or "I know we're focused on Respecting the Absent and that we both want to stick to that, have you talked to your Manager about this yet?"

- Don't participate in any drama. Assume the best intent and encourage your team to be productive in conversations.

By setting this standard, you can avoid unnecessary negativity, foster respect, and keep the team's energy focused on growth rather than distractions.

Ask Yourself:

- Do I allow venting that leads nowhere?

- Do I say things about people that I wouldn't say to them?

- Have I trained my team to Honor the Absent, or do I just hope it happens?

The CPR Method for Tough Conversations

Conflict is inevitable. But when handled well, it becomes a catalyst for growth, not just tension.

I recommend the **CPR Method**, which stands for Connect, Position, and Reset. This framework has helped many leaders I've worked with, and I'm confident it can help you, too. Let's break it down:

Connect - Understand the full story and their perspective.

Position - Share the impact of the behavior on others.

Reset - Collaborate on what comes next.

Connect: First we seek understanding. Ask open-ended questions like, "Can you help me understand what happened here?" or "Could you share more about your perspective on this?" This is a powerful way to get the full context of a situation.

I've learned the hard way assumptions can lead to misunderstandings, so taking time to connect and gather understanding is key.

Once, I went straight into why a team member's actions impacted the team. They'd always been a high performer, but they were showing up late for work, making errors, and weren't as present.

So when I launched into the issues and impacts, I was missing the context. I hadn't asked important questions like, "Can you tell me a bit more about what's going on, inside or outside of work that might be affecting your performance?" or "These issues seem really out of character for you, based on your time here. Can you give me some more information on what's going on from your perspective?"

I learned (after the fact) that this team member's mom was recently diagnosed with cancer. The team member was having a hard time processing this, and it was affecting her day-to-day work. I didn't have the context or tools I needed to help the situation, because I didn't connect with her.

"If you assume that everyone you meet is either in the middle of a crisis or just coming out of one, you'll be right 50% of the time." – Max Lucado.

As leaders, it's our job to make sure we understand what's going on with our team, before we deal with whatever conflict needs addressed. We must be open to seeing the factors that make them human and offer the right tools at the right time. Offering employee assistance programs, walking through what next steps to help them could look like, and making accommodations when needed are helpful. Even offering a 10-minute break to walk outside and gather their thoughts can produce a monumental shift.

Position: This is where you clarify the impact of the issue. What were the consequences for the organization, the team, or even the customer? How did the issue you're addressing affect you personally? By talking through the consequences in a non-emotional way, you keep the conversation constructive and focused on resolution.

This step is difficult for many leaders to master. Some can bring up issues, but they're emotionally charged and they personalize the issue instead of trying to help the team member move forward.

Some don't say anything or give any feedback for long stretches, while hoping things will change, but they burst with frustration when they "reach their limit" and they unload on the team member. Some nitpick and focus on every minor error or issue, trying to control the team member.

Instead, consider what's in the best interest of the team member and the organization. Not just one or the other. By focusing on just the team member, we sometimes overlook issues or make excuses for them, week after week. If we only focus on the organization, we may see that team member as just another cog in the machine. When we focus on both, we strike a compelling balance.

Our goal in this stage isn't to scold or shame, it's to be honest, clear, and constructive. We address the issue with objectivity and care, always aiming for what's best for the team member and the team as a whole.

One of the best pieces of coaching advice I ever got was this:

"My job isn't for you to like everything I say. It's to say what needs to be said, for your benefit. Even when it's hard. Are you open to that?"

That kind of direct but respectful truth-telling can change everything.

When a team member isn't meeting expectations, it impacts others. It adds weight. Frustration. Gaps. This part of the conversation is about helping them *see* that weight so they can take ownership and grow.

But clarity doesn't mean harshness. This isn't about calling someone out. It's about **calling them up**, inviting them to a higher standard with support and belief in their potential.

To do that well, you need to be specific. Do your homework.

- How often has this issue come up?

- What's the ripple effect on the team?

- Are there any missing pieces you still need to understand?

When you walk into that conversation prepared, with facts, empathy, and a clear standard, you give the team member the chance to grow, not just defend.

Reset: After discussing the issue, guide the conversation toward a resolution by asking,

"What do you think we can do to move forward?" or "What's one thing you can commit to doing differently moving forward?"

This allows the person to take ownership of the situation and offer a solution, making it easier for everyone to move forward with a renewed sense of commitment and understanding.

It's ideal for you to have one or two solutions ready to roll out, in case they have nothing to share. It's important to help train your team to come to you with solutions, especially with their own problems.

Those solutions don't need to be great or fully formed to start. The goal is to help them see that their performance and issues are theirs to own and that you, as their coach, are there to guide and support and correct as needed, not take everything on yourself. Trying to "fix" team members and taking over their burdens is one of the best ways to get frustrated, burned out, and keep your team from becoming empowered.

In the Reset step, part of what you want to do is find what fits best for you and the team member. This may mean collaborating on a way to help them become more organized, so they stop missing deadlines. It might involve spending short, focused time each week walking through the best ways to approach team member situations, so they improve communication and prevent conflicts from coming up.

The goal is for them to see and feel that you're on their side, while you maintain your standards.

When done well, the CPR Method doesn't just resolve conflict, it builds maturity, trust, and resilience across your team.

I helped a leader go through this process recently. Her team member was struggling to honor their commitments. They kept taking on too much, intending to get it all done, but their work and quality kept suffering.

The leader dug deeper, asked a few questions, and helped them see how over-committing was actually having the opposite of the desired result. She talked about how it affected the company, the team, and ultimately herself. How it added pressure and stress and took them away from the work that already needed to be done.

Then, the leader said, "With all this in mind, my goal is to help you. I'm right here to help this area of opportunity become one of your best strengths. Are you open to sharing a few thoughts on some ways we can make this better together?"

This approach helped the team member become more receptive to coaching and enabled them to see that their leader was supportive and committed to their growth.

There'll be times, after a few conversations like this, that you and the team member will discover that they may not be a long term fit for the organization. The beautiful part about this process, if done correctly and consistently, is it allows you to express your expectations clearly and effectively along the way. The conversations will focus on the standards, attitudes, and behaviors you must see to help your organization grow. You're inviting them to step into that.

One of my clients walked through this process with a team member and, after a few sessions and progressive coaching, both parties knew it was time for them to move on. As the team member prepared to leave the organization, he said,

"I just want to thank you for how you're letting me go and all the conversations we've had. I know exactly what you've expected, and you've done everything you can to support me. Even though my working here didn't work out, I know all this will help me be a better person in my next spot."

What a powerful exchange. The team member knew the leader had their best interests at heart.

Expect the Best

This final cultural framework supports all the rest. **Expect the Best** means you should always aim to hire the best people, train them well, and encourage them to bring their very best to the table. It's about helping people see their highest potential and coaching them to achieve it. Everyone's "best" is completely individualized, so the goal is to help people reach their fullest potential based on their unique capacities.

I once worked with a leader who had a ton of natural ability. Really smart, quick with conversation, could help others move forward, and.... he was lazy. No, he wasn't "playing video games in his parents' basement" lazy.

He just turned on the laziness whenever he wanted to. Was the CEO and board not looking? Time to turn the laziness on. Was it a concern from the front-line staff about scheduling? Meh, I'll look at the calendar when I have time...

When I addressed this head-on, I focused on expecting the best. I said,

"Tom, I know you're a strong, talented leader. You've helped us so much and you have a ton of potential. And... I don't believe you're giving me and yourself your best."

A look of confusion and anger crossed his face. He reacted immediately:

"What?? You just told me how great of a job I'm doing! I work my tail off here and now you're telling me I'm not working hard enough??"

I gave him a few moments to settle down, so the following words would land a bit deeper. I said,

"Tom, I don't question your help and what you've done here. What I'm addressing is your capacity. Because you're gifted and talented, I believe you have a whole other level to hit.

I believe that your very best looks different than everyone else's. That you can't just skate by and turn your talent on and off whenever you feel like it. Because it's counter to who you are. Everyone has their own strengths and capacity and abilities. What I'm challenging you to do, from here on out, is to look at what your very best is based on. Who you are and who you were made to be.

Are you ready to dig a bit deeper?"

With tears in his eyes, Tom nodded yes.

What I came to discover is that Tom had never been called up like that. He'd been called out, praised, manipulated, and he'd been promised things, but no one had taken the time to tell him the truth and help him really see how what he was doing and not doing impacted those around him.

Tom went on to quickly become one of the best leaders we ever had. His results and consistency improved, but what stood out the most was how he led moving forward. He could confidently call others up, too, helping them expect the best from themselves and others, because he was choosing to do that for himself.

Many of the leaders and organizations change incredibly quickly once they embrace this outlook and framework, first for themselves, and then for their team. Why? Because all of us can always climb another mountain. We can always strive to improve and give our very best, even if it's an area where we've struggled. When we have clear action steps to live out our vision and strive to give our best effort, the results take care of themselves.

Think of one team member who needs to be called up, not called out. What's one conversation you could start today?

Key Takeaways:

Culture is one of the most important aspects of an organization, and the tools we've discussed can help shape a healthy and thriving workplace.

Key Tools for Shaping Culture:

- **Who Is Exercise** – Align identity and purpose

- **The 24-Hour Rule** — Handle conflict quickly and wisely

- **Honor the Absent** — Create safety and accountability

- **CPR Method** — Resolve issues with structure and care

- **Expect the Best** — Raise standards with empathy

Chapter 8: Delivering Magic
How Service Creates Loyalty and Growth

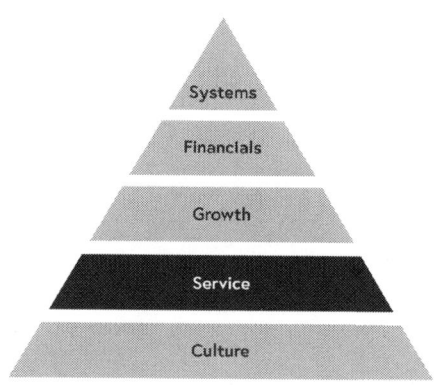

Service starts with the right culture and people, fostering an environment where great service can thrive. Understanding mission-driven service starts with knowing your why, like we covered in the "Who is" exercise. As you move forward, it's critical that every leader in the organization fully understands how your Mission, Vision and Values empower your Service.

Your leadership team is the driver of service success. But don't just take my word for it.

- 70% of employee engagement is driven by managers. This means that employees' attitudes toward customer service are largely shaped by the behavior and leadership style of their managers. (Gallup's State of the American Workplace Report, 2017)

- A separate metric found that employees who see their leaders demonstrate high levels of customer service are 50% more likely to provide exceptional customer service themselves. (McKinsey & Company Research on Leadership in Customer Service, 2020)

- Customer satisfaction levels in these organizations increase by 25% when leadership leads by example. (McKinsey & Company Research on Leadership in Customer Service, 2020)

This research confirms what I've seen in the field, when leaders serve well, everyone rises.

All of this translates into bottom line profit. Organizations with high customer satisfaction have been shown to generate up to 60% higher revenue growth compared to competitors.

So let's dive into 4 actionable frameworks you can use right away with your teams to help improve your top-down service.

Mission Driven Service

When personal values align with the organization's mission, it creates a powerful drive for the team. This becomes essential when challenges arise. A team deeply committed to the mission can overcome conflict and stay focused on the bigger picture. Without a clear mission and Values, teams end up defining the mission for themselves, which can result in misalignment and self-focused goals.

What's your Mission and Values?

I was helping a client recently with their Strategic Planning process. At one point, I asked a simple question:

"What's your Mission Statement, and what does it mean to you?"

What followed was a long pause. Eventually, the CEO broke the silence with a sheepish smile:

"Honestly, I couldn't tell you. None of us really remember it. It's on a plaque somewhere upstairs in the boardroom. It's pretty long... and to be fair, I'm not sure it means much to us anymore."

I hear versions of this all the time. Mission statements and core values that were written years ago, maybe during a retreat or branding exercise, and then forgotten. They don't reflect who the team is today, or where the organization is going.

And when that happens, something powerful is lost. Without a clear, meaningful mission, there's no real North Star. No daily anchor. No shared reason to show up and serve at the highest level. It limits the depth of Mission-Driven Service an organization can offer.

If the mission isn't alive in your people, it can't show up in your work.

"If you want to build a ship, don't drum up the men to gather wood, divide the work, and give orders. Instead, teach them to yearn for the vast and endless sea." - Antoine de Saint-Exupéry

The same is true for any team and organization. A clearly defined mission and set of values completely change the course for any team.

Before I lay out a proven process that will move you into a deeper place of mission-driven service, I want to issue a warning. Going through this process only works if your leadership team is completely bought in and displaying the chosen values consistently.

One sure-fire way to sabotage this process is to have leaders who don't live out the new values.

Teams will follow a leader to the ends of the earth if they consistently display integrity. Otherwise, they'll jump ship as soon as they see choppy waters.

Steps to Develop Mission-Driven Service:

Step 1 – Get your team involved: Get every team member involved. This can look different based on the size of the organization. It could be a meeting for small groups or surveys for larger teams. The goal is to ask the right questions, to pull out what matters most.

Some questions include:

- What values do we display every day here?

- What's the core of what we do?

- What do you hear most from our customers/members that they love the most?

- What drives you daily in your work?

Step 2 – Collect your data and reflect on the trends.

As you review your team's answers, evaluate them from two key perspectives:

What's actual and **what's aspirational**?

What's actual reflects how your team is currently showing up, how they describe the service they give and receive day to day.

What's aspirational reveals what they *hope* to be true, what they value, what they long for, and what great service would look like at its best.

The *actual* helps you see your current reality. The *aspirational* helps you understand the values your team wants to live out, even if they're not fully there yet. These longings can be powerful indicators of what matters most to your people, and what will motivate real change.

Ask questions like:

- Where are we aligned with our values, and where are we falling short?

- What are the recurring themes or gaps?

- Are we providing the kind of internal service that reflects who we say we are?

When you connect those insights, you'll have a clearer roadmap for how to strengthen your culture and build service that's consistent, meaningful, and values-driven.

Step 3 – Craft your updated mission statement and values:

Without doing the pre-work of steps 1 and 2, step 3 can become incredibly difficult. It usually looks like the Executive Team, and perhaps their board, getting away for a day or two, and trying to come up with something that fits their team.

Many ideas are thrown out, and sessions like these often feel like the team just needs to decide on something by the end of the day, even if it doesn't completely fit. I know many clients who've expressed frustration with holding sessions like this before I engaged with them. In fact, one client recently told me their executive team did just that. They held a private retreat and put a new mission statement and values together, all without getting any input from the team.

It flopped. No one was excited or engaged when they rolled it out, and many team members felt shut out of the process. (Don't worry, we're turning this around for them and implementing steps 1 and 2 so they can roll out a collaborative mission and values statement together. It's never too late!)

Share your mission and values: How you roll them out is critical. Some best practices are:

- Have some of your frontline staff and leaders participate in the rollout.

- Share the process everyone went through to help you get here.

- Work with your Marketing team (or resource) to print and visibly display your Mission, Vision, and Values in as many places as possible. This can be visible to your customers/members as well.

- Have an all staff meeting to share how you want these Mission and Values to be lived out each day.

Step 4 – Live your mission and values:

This final step helps you build a Mission Driven Service culture. One of the most common questions I get is, "Now that we've updated our Mission and Vision, how can we make sure we're living this out in our everyday work?" Below are a few targeted ways to make that happen:

1. Incorporate your values into your conversations. One of my client's Mission Statement is "Large Enough to Serve You, Small Enough to Know You." From that one piece we revamped their marketing and growth strategy and identified 4 Core Values that helped drive this Mission.

2. What came out was **Equality, Respect, Trust, Integrity.** Now when they're considering a new promotion or the service they're providing each day, they ask how they're displaying respect to their members. Having your entire team know, speak, and believe in your Mission and Values is core to your success.

3. Once you've rolled out your mission and values, the next challenge is keeping them alive, and that's where service stories become essential.

What Service Stories Highlight Your Values?

Most teams have incredible moments of service, someone going the extra mile for a customer, stepping up for a teammate, or pushing through to complete a project with excellence. But those stories often go untold.

Why? Because to the person doing the work, it just feels like "doing my job." Others may hesitate to speak up because they don't want to brag or think their effort was a big deal.

That's where leadership comes in.

If you want to reinforce your values, you have to surface the stories that show them in action. When your team starts seeing how real-life behavior connects to your mission, values go from words on the wall to something alive in the organization.

How to Surface and Share Service Stories

Many teams struggle to identify great examples, so here's a simple framework:

- **Make it peer-driven**: Ask team members to highlight each other. Most people find it easier to praise a colleague than to talk about their own success.

- **Define what to look for**: Be specific about which values or behaviors you want to see more of. This gives your team a filter for spotting meaningful moments.

- **Make it a rhythm**: Carve out time during weekly or monthly meetings to share stories. Stories lose power if they're shared randomly. They become fuel when shared regularly.

Why This Matters

Great teams can launch quickly. But what keeps them climbing higher, without stalling or crashing, is a steady rhythm of celebration and storytelling.

Why is this so effective?

1. **It proves your values matter**: Real-life stories are the evidence that your mission is more than talk.

2. **It activates pattern recognition**: When you celebrate certain behaviors, like remembering a customer's name or solving an unspoken need, it trains your team to look for more opportunities just like it. (Think of how you suddenly see every Toyota Tundra on the road after shopping for one.)

3. **It creates an emotional lift**: Recognizing service re-energizes people and reminds them their work matters. It's a break from the mundane, and a shot of purpose.

Try This: The "Surprise Spotlight"

This idea has become a favorite with many of my clients.

Here's how it works: Before a meeting, leaders choose one team member to spotlight, but don't tell them. During the meeting, the rest of the team is invited to share short, specific stories of how that person has lived out the mission or shown up in remarkable ways.

It's powerful. It creates a moment of celebration, ownership, and emotional connection, all while reinforcing the behaviors you want more of.

One client started doing this every week at the top of their meetings. Six months later, their team's trust scores were higher than they'd ever seen.

Honoring Others: The Hidden Power of Presence

In leadership, honoring others starts with how we show up: fully present, focused, and intentional.

At its core, honor means treating the person in front of you like they matter most in that moment. In today's fast-paced, always-on world, that kind of presence is rare, but it's also what sets exceptional leaders and teams apart.

Early in my career, I learned this firsthand. I realized that one of the most powerful gifts I could offer someone wasn't a perfect answer or a fast solution, it was my **full attention**. Not distracted. Not rushed. Just fully there, listening, understanding, and connecting.

When I meet with a client, I make small but deliberate choices, silencing my phone, closing my inbox, and turning away from my laptop. That single act of presence often changes the entire tone of the conversation. People feel heard. They feel seen. They feel honored.

And when people feel honored, trust deepens. Service improves. Teams connect. Culture strengthens.

In the sections ahead, we'll get into the specific ways to show honor through nonverbal cues, communication habits, and team-wide behaviors. But it starts here, with the mindset that honoring others begins by being fully present.

How to Honor Others: Practical Ways to Lead with Presence

Now that we've established what it means to honor others, and why presence is so powerful, let's get practical.

Honor shows up in the **small, consistent actions** that leaders and teams take every day. It's in the way we listen, the way we communicate, and how we show people they matter, whether they're a teammate, a customer, or a community partner.

Here are three key ways to put honor into action:

1. Honor with Your Eyes (Be Visually Present)

Whether you're glancing at your phone or scanning the room during a conversation, it sends the message that something, or someone, else is more important.

Try this: when someone is speaking to you, **give them your full eye contact** for at least 30 seconds without distraction. It sounds simple, but it communicates something powerful: *I see you. I value what you're saying.*

2. Honor with Your Body Language (Be Physically Engaged)

Your posture speaks before your words do. Slouching, crossing arms, fidgeting, or turning away can make others feel dismissed or ignored. On the other hand, leaning in, nodding, or mirroring someone's expression signals empathy and interest.

Tip: Use open body language and nods to show you're actively listening. You don't need to say much, your physical presence can do the talking.

3. Honor with Your Time (Be Fully Available, Even Briefly)

Honor doesn't always require long meetings. Sometimes, 5 focused minutes is more meaningful than 30 distracted ones. When a team member, client, or partner approaches you, take a breath, pause what you're doing, and offer them a moment of full availability, even if it's just to say, "I want to give you my full attention. Can we chat in ten minutes?"

Being thoughtful with time is one of the clearest ways to show respect. It tells people:

You're not an interruption. You're the reason we're here.

When your team adopts these habits, everything shifts. Meetings become more focused. Conversations become more meaningful. Trust grows deeper.

And here's the truth: you can't scale a culture of service without a culture of honor.

Honor is the fuel that drives high trust, high performance, and long-term impact. And it starts with how you show up, moment by moment.

Reflection Questions: Are You Leading with Honor?

As you think about how you and your team show up each day, ask yourself:

- When was the last time I gave someone my full, undivided attention?

- What nonverbal signals am I sending in my conversations, am I fully present or partly distracted?

- How do I respond when a team member or customer interrupts my day, do I treat them as an inconvenience or an opportunity?

- Have I set the tone of honor for my team, or am I just hoping it happens?

- What's one small, consistent change I can make this week to show people they matter?

These questions are for action. Honor is a habit, and like any habit, it grows stronger the more intentionally you practice it.

When you model this kind of presence, it becomes contagious, and that's how cultures of honor are built.

Being Honest About When You're Available

I've seen it, and I've been guilty of it, too, leaders trying to multitask or "push through" conversations when they're not really present. Sometimes, it's as simple as needing to take a quick bathroom break or answering an urgent call. Honoring someone's presence means being honest about when you can fully engage in a conversation. If something urgent comes up, it's okay to step away or reschedule. Great leaders don't pile on more and more, ignoring their need to be fully present. Instead, they slow down to reflect and prioritize their time and focus.

Honor Your Word, Actions, and Time

Being clear on who you're serving, why, and how you'll serve them is crucial. It's equally important to honor your commitments. If you constantly say "yes" to everything, you risk over-committing, which leads to diluted service. Over time, this can cause burnout and affect your relationships.

Imagine a line of people waiting for your attention, whether it's your team, your family, or your customers. If someone new jumps to the front, how would everyone else react? Honoring your word means recognizing the impact of your commitments and how they affect others. When we allow someone to jump ahead of the line, we send the message to the current person that their needs are less important, which can harm both our relationships and our ability to deliver great service.

Avoid the Trap of Overcommitment

Service-driven leaders often fall into the trap of saying "yes" to everything, which leads to a dangerous cycle of overcommitment.

By considering every request urgent, we risk neglecting the most important commitments, like developing our teams or maintaining healthy boundaries. Without these boundaries, we end up overwhelmed, and it becomes harder to honor the very people we want to serve.

Take 2 minutes and ask:

What am I overcommitting to that's preventing me from honoring the people who matter most?

Honoring Others by Prioritizing Your Time

Often, leaders take on too many tasks out of a desire to be helpful, but this can overfill your day with tasks that could be handled by others.

I worked with a leader who felt like every request was urgent. As a result, she took on more and more tasks. Her stress levels were rising, and her health and relationships were suffering.

Together, we worked through the following steps:

1. **Inventory of Tasks**: We reviewed her daily, weekly, and monthly tasks and compared them to her strategic priorities, things like one-on-ones, development plans, and strategic planning sessions. We discovered that much of what she was doing wasn't aligned with her highest priorities.

2. **Delegation**: We looked at what tasks could be delegated to others.

In the end, she found that **80% of what she was doing** could be handed off to her team. We started with the easiest tasks that were simple to train her team on.

3. **Reviewing The Calendar**: We examined her calendar to see what commitments or meetings were eating up her time, preventing her from focusing on higher-level service and honoring her commitments effectively.

The result?

She freed up **5 hours per week** by delegating tasks and making time for the most important work. After implementing these changes, she said, "I never thought I could actually feel on top of things and take care of myself and my team at the same time."

Since then, she, and many other leaders we've worked with, have seen improved internal service scores, better communication within their teams, and the ability to coach their teams more effectively, just by focusing on what matters most.

Key Takeaways:

1. **Be present**: Honoring others starts with giving them your full attention. Set aside distractions like phone notifications, emails, and multitasking to show that you value a person's time.

2. **Communicate nonverbally**: Over half of communication is nonverbal. When you're present, you can better understand both what's said and what's left unsaid.

3. **Be honest about your availability**: Recognize when you're able to give someone your full attention, and be honest if something urgent comes up that requires you to step away.

The Rule of 7's - Why Perfect Practice Builds Real Confidence

There's a myth in business that great service or communication is instinctive. That people are either "naturals" or they're not. The truth? Excellence is practiced. And not just practiced, but practiced with intention.

That's where the **Rule of 7's** comes in.

This framework is simple: before launching something new, whether it's a team interaction, a presentation, or a new customer process, you practice it *seven times*. Repetition builds confidence. And not just the appearance of confidence, but real internal conviction and capability.

Why Seven?

Psychologist George Miller's famous study found that our brains tend to hold about 7 chunks of information at a time. That number pops up again and again in memory and learning science, and for good reason. 7 reps is often just enough to work out the kinks, build comfort with a process, and shift from just knowing the idea to *owning* it.

But here's the key: **it's not just about repetition, it's about perfect practice**. Lazy reps reinforce lazy habits. Focused reps build mastery.

When I coach leaders, I've used this framework to help them prepare for everything from executive meetings to customer escalations. I've seen the shift firsthand: leaders who were nervous or inconsistent at first become clear, confident, and composed, just through intentional reps.

What to Practice? Just About Everything.

The Rule of 7's applies to almost any part of your work:

- Rolling out a new service standard? Practice it.

- Preparing for a high-stakes pitch or board presentation? Practice it.

- Coaching a direct report through a tough conversation? Practice it.

Every repetition builds muscle memory, and with it, mental clarity.

How to Make Your 7 Reps Count

Not all practice is created equal. Here are 3 practical ways to elevate your reps and build real capability:

1. Role-Playing - Practice Under Pressure Simulate real-world conversations in a low-risk environment. Whether it's a customer complaint, a hiring interview, or a coaching moment, walking through these scenarios out loud helps teams build the confidence and responsiveness they'll need when it counts.

2. Scripting - Prepare, Then Pivot Write out key talking points or opening lines for high-stakes moments. This isn't about sounding robotic, it's about being ready. Once the core message is locked in, practice adjusting in real time so your delivery stays human and flexible.

3. Coaching - Get Outside Eyes on Your Gaps Feedback accelerates growth. Invite someone to listen, watch, or even record your practice. Whether it's a colleague, a coach, or just your phone camera, seeing yourself through another lens can reveal blind spots and spark fast improvement.

The Power of Real Preparation

I've seen teams transform their service delivery just by implementing this mindset. One group I worked with used the Rule of 7's to rehearse their responses to common service challenges. The difference between their first run and their seventh was night and day, better clarity, smoother delivery, and way more confidence.

Even better, when the real challenges came up in the field, the reps didn't freeze or fumble. They knew exactly what to do, because they'd already done it.

Key Takeaways

- **Practice with purpose**. Seven focused reps help embed new skills and build comfort before it's time to perform.

- **Use tools like scripting, role-playing, and coaching** to sharpen your delivery and anticipate curveballs.

- **Perfect practice beats blind repetition**. Each run-through should be a chance to improve, not just repeat.

10:1 Praise to Correction Ratio

People respond well to genuine, positive reinforcement. Research by Dr. B. F. Skinner, a pioneer in behavioral psychology, showed that positive reinforcement is one of the most powerful motivators for changing behavior. When people feel recognized and appreciated, they're more likely to continue those behaviors.

A Gallup study found that employees who receive regular praise are 14% more engaged in their work. Because engagement is linked to productivity, higher engagement directly translates into better service delivery and business results.

This positive reinforcement needs to be specific. How did they preserve through a tough situation? How did they help a customer feel through their kindness? Get specific on what you saw, what type of character they displayed, and what kind of impact it made. Just giving out a few "great jobs" or "nice work" won't make any lasting impact.

When team members feel valued, they develop confidence, which makes them more motivated to perform well. According to a study by the American Psychological Association, employees praised for their efforts are 20% more likely to take initiative and seek out challenges, compared to those who receive little or no positive feedback. This increased initiative helps drive service excellence.

Constructive feedback is still critical for improvement, and balance is key. Too much correction can make employees feel like they're always falling short. They might lose the motivation to keep improving. When you strike the right balance, lots of praise and just enough correction, you create an environment where people feel supported, valued, and inspired to perform at their best.

You also help reinforce the standard for what you want to see more of, just by highlighting the good. I had one client who took this challenge on with her team. She confessed that she naturally saw more issues than positives in her team's work and their culture reflected this. They had lower scores in trust and feeling cared for overall, which affected morale and productivity.

So, she focused on the good. She studied the areas going well and highlighted them. She acknowledged good behaviors and character each day. It wasn't forced or fake. She just set an intention to do this a few times per day with her teams and highlight it in specific ways. A targeted message in a team meeting, a quick, specific thank you in the hallway, a constructive positive message through text.

The results were amazing! In less than 3 months, she saw her team's engagement, productivity, and overall care skyrocket (all 3 had over a 20% increase on average).

She later shared,

*"Michael, it's like we have an all-new office, and it really started with what I was focusing on. **The more I focused on the good, the more the team rose to meet that standard.** Sure, we still have issues pop up that we must fix, but way less than before. It's like the team is self-identifying when they're*

going above and beyond and highlighting it in each other as well. Everyone loves working here now."

The 3 Components of Effective Praise

To really make an impact, focus your praise on:

- **Effort: Praise grit, persistence, and showing up**

Recognizing someone's hard work and determination is powerful. When people feel like their efforts are seen, they're more likely to keep pushing forward. This is supported by Carol Dweck's research on the "growth mindset," which shows that praising effort rather than innate talent fosters a mindset of continual improvement and resilience. In fact, Dweck found that people praised for effort were **60% more likely** to tackle new challenges, while those praised for innate ability were more likely to avoid challenges they might fail at.

- **Behavior: Call out actions that align with values**

Praise the actions that align with your values and goals. If an employee goes the extra mile to help a customer or solves a tough problem, point it out and reinforce it. A study published in the Journal of Applied Psychology found that **employees who were recognized for specific behaviors saw a 27% increase** in their overall performance. Recognizing positive behavior contributes to team unity, as it encourages others to copy those actions.

- **Character: Highlight integrity, teamwork, humility, resilience**

Recognize the traits that make people good at their jobs, whether it's patience, teamwork, or problem-solving. Acknowledging these qualities helps reinforce what matters most in a workplace culture. Research by Gallup highlights that organizations that focus on employees' strengths (like character traits) experience **an average of 14.9% higher profitability** and **18% higher productivity**. Praising these intrinsic qualities contributes not only to individual growth but also to the overall success of the organization.

Key Takeaways:

1. **Praise should outweigh correction:** Aim for **10 positive instances** for every correction you give. Remember, studies show that employees who receive regular praise are **14% more engaged** and more productive.

2. **Praise drives motivation**: It boosts confidence and encourages people to keep improving. Research shows that employees praised for effort are **20% more likely** to take on new challenges, which directly translates into higher performance.

3. Focus your praise on **effort, behavior, and character,** which helps reinforce the right actions and creates an environment of positive growth. Organizations that focus on strengths and behavior recognition see higher profitability and productivity.

The more specific you are with praise, the more scalable your culture becomes. Great service starts by recognizing the right things, consistently.

Chapter 9: The Growth Engine
The Secret To Sustainable Scaling

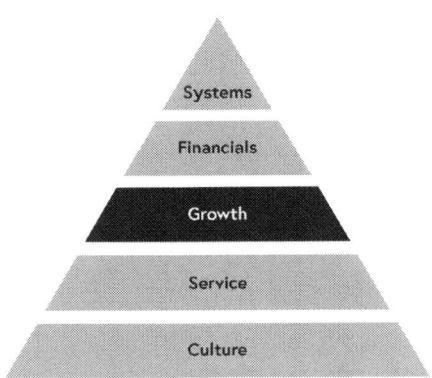

One of my clients led a company that got off to a hot start. They had low competition in the marketplace, had a good culture and prided themselves on service. The problem was that after about 18 months, after everyone settled in, their growth started to fade. It was slow at first, but as each quarter passed, they saw their sales start to slip.

This led them to focus on their numbers even harder. At every meeting, one-on-one, and almost every email, they shared where they weren't and figured communicating the growing gap in their company's performance would help light a fire under everyone in the organization.

Guess what? It didn't.

In fact, it had the opposite effect and caused their results to drop even more.

Why?

Because while growth is the ultimate goal for any business, it can quickly become misguided when it's focused solely on numbers. When businesses chase after figures like sales targets and market share without investing in the right foundational elements we've discussed, growth becomes unsustainable. This often leads to boom-and-bust cycles that create frustration and burnout.

If you want to avoid the "burnout loop" and build growth that scales, here are three frameworks that transform your team from reactive to focused and fired up: **The Game of Work**, **Recommendation-Based Selling (RBS)**, and **Development Plans**. Each of these frameworks is designed to foster engagement, build accountability, and drive success for both individuals and organizations as a whole.

The Game of Work - Turning Growth into a Team Sport

One of the biggest mistakes I see leaders make is assuming their team is just as motivated by growth as they are.

The reality? If growth is only tracked in terms of sales, profit margins, net income, numbers your team can't influence or even fully understand, it creates distance. Leaders may feel passionate, but the team often feels disconnected, unclear, and unmotivated.

If you want lasting growth, you need something better than targets on a whiteboard. You need a framework that gets everyone playing the same game, with the same energy.

What Is the Game of Work?

Charles Coonradt coined the idea in his book *The Game of Work*, and it's simple but powerful: if you want your people to perform at a high level, treat work like a game, with clear rules, a visible scoreboard, and measurable ways to win.

Without those elements, people just go through the motions.

I once worked with a client whose team wasn't engaged at all in the company's growth.

Here's what we found:

- Team bonuses were tied to annual metrics, things like net income or expense ratios, that no one fully understood.

- No one knew how to impact those numbers day to day.

- They didn't know how they were doing until the year was over.

- So, the bonus felt like luck. Not effort.

Can you blame them for checking out?

As Coonradt says, *"Without a scoreboard, employees can't engage with their work in a meaningful way."*

Why the Game Works

People need to see how they're doing. In sports, players wouldn't take the game seriously without a scoreboard. The same goes for work. Without clear tracking, your team loses motivation and ownership, two things essential to sustainable growth.

That's what the Game of Work solves.

You give people something they can see, control, and win at, something that aligns with your business goals–and suddenly they care. Because now they know how to win.

How It Works: Making Success Measurable and Visible

I worked with a credit union that wanted to improve growth, but the team felt stuck. So we created a visible scoreboard built around a behavior they *could* control: having more financial conversations.

We broke it down like this:

- **Every team member** had a goal for how many financial conversations they'd have each day.

- **Frontline staff** had a higher number due to more member interaction.

- **Back-office teams** had lower but still meaningful goals, at events, with friends, or through community outreach.

Each team tracked their numbers using a method that worked for them, whiteboards, spreadsheets, or daily check-ins. It didn't matter how, it mattered that they tracked it.

And within 6 months?

- **New member growth:** up 45%

- **Loan growth:** up 34%

- **Deposit growth:** up 32%

They weren't just doing more, they were doing what mattered most. And they knew it.

The Science of Scoreboards

This approach is backed by research:

- A Harvard Business Review study found that companies with clear performance metrics saw a **32% boost in productivity**.

- According to Gallup, employees who understand how their role contributes to success are **21% more productive** than those who don't.

I've helped dozens of organizations install simple scoreboards tied to the behaviors that move the needle, and every time, engagement and growth improve.

Because when people know what to do, how to track it, and how it connects to something bigger, they show up differently.

The Ripple Effect

When a team sees that their efforts are moving the scoreboard, it creates momentum. Not just in the numbers, but in culture:

- **Engagement increases** because people feel a sense of ownership.

- **Turnover drops** because team members know they matter.

- **Teamwork improves** because everyone's aiming for the same goal.

At that credit union, people started celebrating each other more. They asked questions like, *"How many conversations did you have today?"* Not to compete, but to encourage. Because now they had language and structure around what success looked like, and they were all in.

The Big Idea

Coonradt says it best: *"The Game of Work is about ensuring that every player knows the rules, sees the scoreboard, and is motivated to win together."*

This is what great leadership looks like. Giving people a scoreboard they can believe in, and then coaching them to win, together.

Key Takeaways

- **Define the rules.** Clarify what specific actions lead to success. Make sure your team knows how they can personally contribute to the win.

- **Build a visible scoreboard.** Track progress in real time, whether on a whiteboard, spreadsheet, or daily huddle. Visibility drives ownership.

- **Celebrate progress.** The more people feel seen and successful, the more they'll show up and give their best.

- **Focus on behaviors, not just outcomes.** When you track what your team can *control*, the results will follow.

Recommendation-Based Selling (RBS) - From Pitching to Partnering

At its core, great sales is about alignment. And yet, so many teams struggle with it.

What Gets in the Way of Great Sales?

I've seen it across industries: talented teams hesitate to sell because they feel uneasy. Maybe they've had bad experiences with high-pressure tactics.

Maybe they're unsure how to talk about your product without sounding scripted or salesy. Or maybe, and this is a big one, they don't fully believe in what they're offering.

That hesitation shows up in lost opportunities, missed goals, and flat energy during client interactions.

According to recent studies, **57% of salespeople miss their quotas** because they're not confident in how to connect value to customer needs.

If your team isn't excited about what they're offering, you can't expect customers to be.

The Shift: From Selling to Recommending

Recommendation-Based Selling (RBS) is a consultative approach that turns your team from reluctant sellers into trusted advisors.

Here's the shift:

- From scripts to conversations

- From pitching to problem-solving

- From pressure to partnership

RBS works because it taps into something your team is already doing, recommending. We naturally recommend our favorite restaurants, shows, and vacation spots. RBS helps your team apply that same mindset to your product or service. When they believe in it, and understand how it solves problems, it becomes easy, and even energizing, to talk about.

How to Build RBS into Your Sales Culture:

1. Set Clear Expectations for the Conversation

Before diving into questions or offers, set the tone. Let the customer know you're there to help, not to sell.

This can be casual and friendly, like:

- "Would it be crazy if I asked you a financial question as part of our time today?"

- "As part of your visit, I'd love to ask a couple quick questions to see if we can save you some money. Sound good?"

This lowers defenses and gives your team permission to explore needs without feeling pushy.

Why it works: Forrester found that **74% of customers are more engaged** when they know what's coming next. Clear expectations build trust and reduce resistance.

2. Ask Better Questions During Discovery

Once expectations are set, shift into **discovery**. This is where your team uncovers real needs, and builds real connections.

Encourage open-ended questions like:

- "What's one of your financial goals this year?"

- "If you could wave a magic wand and eliminate one financial stress, what would it be?"

These questions lead to richer conversations and more opportunities to help. They move your team beyond the script into something more authentic, and more effective.

Sales reps who ask **5 or more discovery questions** are 3.5x more likely to close the deal (HubSpot).

3. Make Tailored Recommendations Based on Their Answers

This could sound like:

- "Based on what you've shared, I'd recommend our secured loan. It's helped a lot of members in your situation consolidate their debt quickly and affordably. Want to see how it could work for you?"

- "From what you told me, I'd suggest we create a plan to help you improve energy efficiency and lower your monthly bills. We've helped dozens of clients do just that. Want me to show you how it works?"

This sounds natural because it *is* natural. We recommend things we believe in every day. The key is helping your team make that mental shift from *selling* to *serving*.

Why RBS Works Across Any Industry

This approach works in banking, insurance, education, manufacturing, and even lawn care because people everywhere respond to genuine help over generic hype.

I've watched teams implement RBS and consistently see **17% to 34% growth in just 3 months**.

The key is **practice and belief**. When your team buys in, when they understand the value and feel equipped to talk about it, they become your biggest promoters.

The results speak for themselves:

- Companies using consultative selling see **26% higher win rates**

- And **33% better customer retention**

RBS turns conversations into conversions, and conversions into loyalty.

Key Takeaways:

- **Set the tone early:** Get permission to ask questions and clarify your intent, to help, not just to sell.

- **Ask thoughtful, open-ended questions:** Discover the real challenges behind the request. The better your team listens, the better they'll connect.

- **Recommend, don't pitch:** Tailor suggestions based on what the customer actually needs. Use language that feels conversational, not salesy.

- **Build belief through repetition:** Confidence comes from clarity and practice. Train, coach, and model it until it becomes second nature.

Development Plans - Turning Growth from Concept to Commitment

What's the difference between good intentions and actual growth? A written plan.

Development plans turn potential into progress. They provide structure, direction, and accountability, so team members don't just talk about growing, they actually do it.

Without a plan, development is vague. Goals get forgotten. Momentum fades. But with a clear, written development plan, especially one built on a 90-day cycle, growth becomes part of the rhythm of work.

And when done right, it doesn't just benefit the individual. It strengthens the entire team and builds a culture of progress.

Why 90 Days?

A 90-day plan gives your team a clear runway to make meaningful progress without getting overwhelmed. It's long enough to see change, but short enough to stay urgent.

- According to Stanford research, **only 3% of people have written goals**, but those who do are **10x more likely to succeed**.

- LinkedIn found that **93% of employees would stay longer** at a company that invests in their development.

- Dominican University research shows that people are **42% more likely to reach their goals** when they're written down.

The numbers are clear: when team members know where they're going, how to get there, and that someone's supporting them along the way, they thrive.

What a Development Plan Actually Looks Like

Development plans are commitments that lay out:

- Clear goals

- Specific action steps

- Timelines

- Ownership from the team member

They can be driven by performance conversations, or initiated by the employee, but they should always be part of the regular rhythm of leadership, not something saved for annual reviews or check-the-box moments.

I've seen great leaders use development plans to help their top talent grow even stronger, and also to reignite team members who felt stuck or disconnected. When used well, a development plan becomes a tool for both clarity and care.

How to Build a 90-Day Development Plan (In 3 Phases)

Phase 1: Set the Goals and Frame the Journey

Start with a focused conversation about strengths, goals, and areas of opportunity. Ask:

- Where is this team member already showing potential?

- What would help them take the next step forward?

- What would success look like 90 days from now?

You're helping build the blueprint here, not pointing them to a promotion or "next role," but focusing on how they can **bloom where they're planted** and become the best version of themselves right where they are.

Phase 2: Collaborate and Refine

This step is about alignment. You and the team member work together to adjust the plan based on capacity, timing, and relevance.

According to Gallup, team members who **co-create their development plan** are **70% more likely to stay engaged** with it.

This isn't something you do *for* them. It's something you build *with* them. The more ownership they have, the more likely they'll follow through.

Phase 3: Ownership with Support

Once the plan is finalized, the team member leads the process. You check in, coach as needed, and help them troubleshoot. But they're the driver now, not you.

Harvard Business Review found that employees who **own their growth** are **2.5x more likely** to perform at a high level.

If you feel like you're dragging the plan forward, it's a signal something's off. Revisit the goals, the clarity, or the accountability, and reset as needed.

Key Takeaways - Growth That Sticks

- **Clarity:** Give your team a visible scoreboard. Make success tangible. When people can see how their daily actions move the needle, they become more engaged, more motivated, and more accountable. Clear goals = consistent momentum.

- **Alignment:** Help your team shift from selling to solving. When they understand the customer's needs and believe in your product, they move from pressure to partnership. RBS builds trust, confidence, and long-term results, for your team and your clients.

- **90-Day Development Plans:** When your team members write their goals, co-create their action steps, and take ownership of their growth, everything changes. You move from vague hopes to focused action. And over time, that creates a culture of continuous improvement.

Chapter 10: Profit with Purpose
Where to Invest for Maximum Momentum

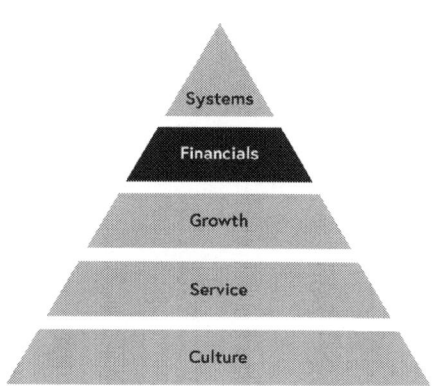

Once growth is in motion, a new question emerges: **What will you do with it?**

That's where profit meets purpose.

When your business hits a season of financial success, it's easy to focus on short-term gains. But sustainable growth demands intentional reinvestment, a commitment to generosity, and scalable systems that save time and increase impact.

In this chapter, we'll walk through three essential strategies that turn profits into long-term momentum:

1. Reinvesting profits to free up time and fuel growth

2. Incorporating generosity to build reputation and trust

3. Setting clear giving goals that reflect your core values

Reinvesting Profits to Free Up Time and Fuel Growth

When growth hits, it's exciting, but it can also create new complexity. The question is: **Are you building something that scales, or something that just gets heavier?**

Our clients often see a 20% to 35% increase in profits within their first year of implementing this framework. That growth comes from the foundational work done in the Culture, Service, and Growth phases.

But what happens next determines if that success will last.

Why Reinvestment Matters

The smartest reinvestment strategies don't just add more, they **multiply**. They empower your team, improve efficiency, and save time that can be spent on innovation and impact.

This is about **leveraging tools and training to make your business stronger, faster, and more scalable**.

When reinvestment is intentional, profits become a flywheel, not just a finish line.

How to Decide Where to Invest

Take a step back and ask:

"If we had an extra $100k this year, what investment would help us fulfill our mission and values most effectively?"

This isn't just about ROI in the traditional sense. It's about return on **impact**, on your team, your time, your customer experience, and your long-term momentum.

Too often, profits get funneled into pet projects, saved indefinitely, or scattered without a strategy. Having financial reserves is smart. But if you're not aligning your profit with your mission, you're missing one of your biggest levers for growth.

Two Mindsets. Two Outcomes.

I once worked with a business owner who viewed profit as something to extract, not reinvest. He resisted updating systems or training leaders, even as the company faltered. The result? Shrinking profits, low morale, and talks of selling the business just to stay afloat.

Compare that to another client who made reinvestment a consistent part of their strategy. Each year, he set aside funds to train their leaders and streamline team operations. He asked questions like:

"What can we do to make your work more efficient?" "How can we improve our customer experience with the resources we have?"

The results?

- Net income consistently between 20–30%

- Near-zero turnover

- A team that's fully engaged and empowered

The difference between these two leaders wasn't access to profit. It was their **philosophy of reinvestment**.

The ROI of Generosity: Giving That Fuels Growth

If you're only chasing profit, you may find yourself in a cycle of unsustainable practices that miss the deeper purpose of business, which is serving others and creating value. When businesses prioritize giving, whether that's through charitable efforts, team member benefits, or community involvement, they see positive results not only in their internal culture but also in their bottom line over time.

Honoring Impact and Generosity

By reinvesting profits into the community or causes that align with your values, you create goodwill, foster trust, and strengthen relationships with customers, team members, and partners. This builds a foundation of loyalty and support that can drive sustainable growth.

Finances can also allow for what's called Radical Generosity. This is where your business gets creative with your giving, to allow others to know more about you and what you love to do in the community.

Radical Generosity Examples:

- Buy everyone's coffee for an hour

- Fill gas tanks with no strings attached

- Pay for groceries at checkout unexpectedly

I've helped dozens of organizations put together some creative Radical Generosity activities, and a few amazing things always happen. Team members are so grateful to be a part of something creative and special that they always want to help at the next event.

The community and partnering businesses love it. People decide to do business or apply for work at the businesses practicing Radical Generosity because it activates something deep in them.

In fact, one person came in to apply for a position and sign up for an account at one of my client's businesses simply because of how his mom was treated. We'd purchased gas for her the day before. He said,

"Anyone who's willing to help serve my mom like that, with no strings attached, deserves my business and is someone I want to work for."

The Law of Sowing and Reaping

By giving, you plant seeds that will grow long after the moment has passed.

Over time, businesses that give without expecting anything in return build reputations that attract loyal customers and dedicated team members. According to a study from Cone Communications, **87% of consumers will purchase from a company that supports a cause they care about.**

Giving also helps businesses stand out in a crowded marketplace. It's a privilege to earn and give back. What's true in farming holds true for every organization. The more you sow into your people, into your community, and into giving back in the right ways, the more resources you'll receive long term to continue the process and increase your harvests.

I'm not saying to give just to get.

The goal is to give and recognize that our generosity will result in more to give as we continue to sow. It's the law of the harvest.

Building Long-Term Value Through Strategic Reinvestment

Profit isn't powerful unless it's planned. Strategic reinvestment ensures today's success becomes tomorrow's stability.

Just like other key business objectives, reinvestment should be intentional and measurable. One of the issues I see with certain businesses is a lack of planning for this reinvestment or deviating from their plans when times are good. It's an easy trap to fall into. When everything looks strong, it's tempting to deviate from your reinvestment goals, assuming that your level of profitability and net income will always stay steady.

An article by Forbes titled *How To Know If You're Reinvesting In Your Business Effectively*, suggests that small businesses consider reinvesting **20-50%** of their profits to drive growth, particularly in areas such as marketing, technology, and staffing. The article stresses that the percentage will vary depending on business goals and growth stages, but a consistent reinvestment strategy is key to long-term success.

- **Scaling and Strengthening Systems:** A strong operational foundation can help you adapt to market shifts, improve efficiency, and stay ahead of competition, all of which contribute to sustained growth.

- **Anticipating Future Needs:** By setting aside funds for unforeseen needs, your business can remain agile and ready. This strategic foresight ensures that your company doesn't just survive but thrives, even in uncertain times.

- **Long-Term Benefits of Reinvestment:** Companies that consistently reinvest in their growth often see stronger market positioning, better talent retention, and improved customer loyalty. Studies show that businesses investing strategically in growth initiatives see up to 25% higher revenue growth over 5 years compared to those that don't.

By reinvesting in systems, tools, and team development, you can increase operational efficiency and free up your time to focus on strategic initiatives.

What's one area in your business where reinvestment could have the biggest impact over the next 12 months?

Write it down, and make a plan to take action.

Chapter 11: Systems that Last
Building Success That Doesn't Depend on You

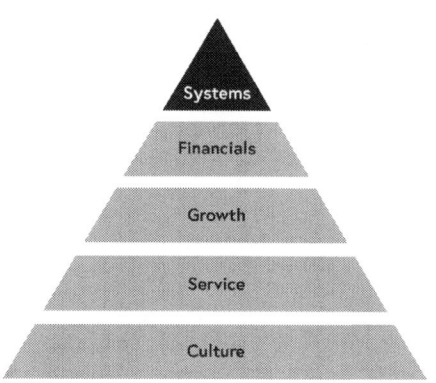

Systems, technology, and processes change constantly. Just think about how different business looked 5 years ago. To adapt as you evolve, your systems must be based on a strong foundation of culture, service, growth, and financial clarity.

This is why I'm such a proponent of frameworks. They're not rigid. They mold and scale with your team. They aren't dependent on a single technology, person, or season. They provide consistency and flexibility, two essentials for lasting success.

I've been there. The new software, CRM, or "all-in-one" solution sounds amazing, and sometimes it is. But no system can solve all your problems. It can only enhance what already works.

Once your Culture, Service, Growth, and Finances are strong, you're ready for systems that scale.

Organizing the Funnel

To make success scalable, start by looking at where decisions, tasks, and information get stuck, and begin clearing the funnel.

The Role of the Leader

Too often, leaders become the funnel. Everything runs through them, approvals, decisions, meetings, updates, and eventually, it clogs the flow.

Instead, create a streamlined flow of work where you're not the catch-all for every task, decision, and bottleneck.

Instead of being the funnel, you want to become the hourglass. While everything may flow through you, your role is to narrow the focus, clarify direction, and then distribute responsibility back out.

What keeps leaders stuck in the funnel?

- They can't say no. They've trained their teams, board, or stakeholders to come to them for everything.

- They like doing other people's work. It feels good to jump in and "get things done," even if it's not your task anymore.

- They haven't trained or developed their team. They hold onto tasks out of fear it won't be done "the right way."

Sound familiar?

If so, you're not alone, and you're not stuck.

Let's walk through a system to free up your time, develop your team, and scale your success.

4 Steps to Build Systems That Scale

These are the 4 steps I use with clients to create clarity, free up time, and reclaim leadership energy. Leaders who implement these typically get **5 to 10 hours back per week**, and build stronger workflows in the process.

Step 1: Time Audits - Reclaiming Hours on Your Calendar

Start by identifying which tasks consume time but aren't aligned with your core role. Studies show that 45% of employees spend over ten hours a week on tasks that could be delegated.

One leader who did this exercise realized she was spending over **9 hours a week** on tasks that her team should've been handling. She had taken them on "just to help," but never gave them back.

Her audit revealed a hard truth: **she was owning work that no longer belonged to her**.

Within 3 weeks, she trained her team to own those tasks and reports again. She told me:

"Michael, I just freed up 9 hours per week! I was working 50 to 55 hours consistently and feeling stressed out. Now I'm coaching my team and finally focusing on the parts of leadership I love."

That's the power of a time audit.

Evaluate your daily, weekly, monthly, and quarterly activities. Ask:

- Is this still mine to do?

- Could this be delegated after training and clear direction?

Your goal is to hold onto the strategic functions: one-on-ones, planning, team development, coaching, and high-level execution.

Step 2: Delegation - How to Leverage Your Team

Delegation empowers people. Organizations that delegate effectively see a **25% increase in engagement**.

One key barrier? Leaders don't realize how much stress they're passing on.

If you're constantly saying how busy or overloaded you are, your team will mirror it. They'll avoid asking for help. Or worse, they'll carry your stress without clarity or structure.

One of the best questions you can ask is:

"On a scale of 1 to 10, how full is your plate right now?"

Use the answer to dig deeper:

- What are they actually working on?

- Do they have the systems to support it?

- Is the workload temporary or ongoing?

Most teams are more capable than leaders think. They just need coaching, clarity, and trust. When that happens, the leader stops being the bottleneck and becomes the multiplier.

Step 3: Boundaries - Don't Treat Everything as Urgent

Everything can't be urgent. And when everything feels urgent, your focus disappears.

Without a priority system, you'll either:

- Panic and treat everything as high-stakes

- Burn out and stop responding to anything

Here's a simple system I teach leaders to filter priorities:

Critical: Must-do this week. No negotiation.

Urgent: Due in 1–3 weeks. Schedule and plan.

Important: Future-focused ideas or initiatives. Great, but not immediate.

One leader I worked with applied this and immediately felt relief. We dumped his 47-task to-do list into these three buckets, and within a week, he was making faster, better decisions.

If you're feeling overwhelmed, try the **Prioritization Drill**:

Take 5 minutes, list everything you're carrying, and sort it into these three buckets. You'll be amazed how much clarity it brings.

Step 4: Time Blocking - Create a Power Hour That Works

Research shows that using **time-blocking** improves productivity by up to **40%**.

Start simple:

- Block 15 minutes of focused time

- Silence your phone

- Turn off email

- Work on one task only

Keep a notepad nearby for intrusive thoughts, but stay focused.

Over time, build up to a full **Power Hour**: a 45-minute block of uninterrupted deep work followed by a short break.

Use your most energized time of day, morning for most people. Let your team know you're in "focus mode" and define what qualifies as urgent during that time.

When leaders do this, their productivity goes up. Their stress goes down. And their team starts to mirror the behavior.

Consistent One-on-Ones - Creating Space for Growth Conversations

These meetings aren't for status updates or solving emergencies. They're for:

- Coaching

- Feedback

- Development

They show your team you're **invested in their success**.

According to Gallup, 84% of employees say regular one-on-ones improve their performance and job satisfaction.

Make them structured and intentional:

- Review goals and development plans

- Offer praise and constructive feedback

- Discuss career growth

- Address challenges proactively

Regular one-on-ones create rhythm, alignment, and trust. They keep small issues from becoming big ones, and turn good people into great performers.

Strategic Planning - From Document to Driving Force

The next layer is your **Strategic Plan**. But it can't just be a one-time exercise. It must become a **living roadmap**.

Only 12% of companies have a truly effective strategic plan. Most fail because they're either too vague, too ambitious, or disconnected from day-to-day work.

Building a Plan That Actually Works

Start with buy-in. Survey your leaders, team, and board before you plan. Ask:

- What's working?

- What's not?

- What should we do more or less of?

Anchor it to the Big Five:

Culture, Service, Growth, Finances, Systems. Set 3-year goals for each. Break them down into quarterly action steps.

- Assign owners. Every initiative needs someone responsible.

- Name an Action Owner and an Accountability Partner for each major goal.

- Adapt as you grow. Review progress quarterly. Update based on reality, not just your ideal timeline.

A plan only works if you review it, use it, and adjust it consistently.

A strategic plan, when executed well, becomes the heartbeat of your organization, aligning every action to your mission and driving measurable progress.

Research from Harvard Business Review shows that companies with dynamic, regularly updated strategic plans achieve 25% higher revenue growth over five years compared to those with static or nonexistent plans.

Consider the story of a mid-sized manufacturing firm I worked with that was struggling with inconsistent performance. Their leadership team had a vision but no clear roadmap to connect daily operations to long-term goals.

By implementing a strategic plan anchored to the Big Five, with quarterly reviews and clear action owners, they saw a 30% increase in operational efficiency within 18 months.

More importantly, their team reported higher clarity and engagement, as everyone understood how their work contributed to the bigger picture. A living strategic plan doesn't just guide your business - it energizes it, turning vision into reality with every step.

Succession Planning - Building for the Future

Strategic planning helps today. **Succession planning** secures tomorrow.

It ensures you're prepared when people move on, whether by choice or chance.

A great plan includes:

- Key positions and their backups

- Readiness ratings

- Development needs

- Timelines for transition

I've seen great organizations fail because one key leader left and no one knew what came next. I've also seen teams thrive during leadership changes because they had the right plan in place.

Build a **Succession Tracker** you can review quarterly. That clarity changes everything. The tracker should include key positions and provide a dashboard to help you see all the data referenced above. It should ideally be updated every 6 months to help keep your planning efforts on track.

Succession planning is not just about filling roles—it's about building a legacy of leadership that sustains your organization's momentum.

According to Korn Ferry, organizations with robust succession plans are 33% more likely to maintain leadership effectiveness during transitions, ensuring stability and growth.

I once worked with a credit union facing the retirement of their long-time CEO. Without a succession plan, they risked losing direction and trust.

By creating a detailed Succession Tracker, identifying internal talent, and investing in targeted development, they seamlessly transitioned to a new CEO who had been mentored for the role over two years.

The result?

A 20% increase in member growth and zero disruption in operations. Effective succession planning empowers your team, builds confidence in the future, and ensures your culture and vision endure, no matter who's at the helm.

Technology - Support, Not the Solution

Don't let the shiny new tool steal the spotlight from the real work. I've seen too many teams ditch perfectly good systems because leaders didn't bother to ask what their people needed or failed to train them on the new solution. Start with your team's input. What's slowing them down? Where's the friction? Choose technology that smooths those rough edges. When done right, tech can slash manual tasks by 40% and boost efficiency across the board. But let's be clear: technology is never the star of the show. It's a supporting actor, amplifying the culture, service, and growth you've already built.

When It Still Feels Hard - Common Roadblocks

Even with rock-solid systems, you'll hit bumps. That's not failure—it's growth in action. Here's what to watch for and how to push through:

- **Heroing**: Trying to do it all yourself. It leads to burnout and bottlenecks. → **Fix**: Equip your team and trust them to lead. Let go so they can step up.

- **Poor Delegation**: Handing off tasks without clarity, training, or expectations. → **Fix**: Use SMART goals, provide coaching, and build accountability loops that stick.

- **No Process**: Everyone doing things their own way, creating chaos. → **Fix**: Design clear, step-by-step workflows. Turn recurring mess into repeatable clarity.

Here's the truth: you're not meant to carry the load alone. Be a guide, not a sherpa. Show the way forward, and let your team own the journey.

Systems That Scale - Final Thoughts

Great systems don't just keep the lights on—they set your team free to thrive. When your systems are strong, your people are empowered to do their best work, your business runs like a well-tended garden, and you're no longer stuck putting out fires.

You're leading with vision, coaching with purpose, and building something that lasts. Imagine a team that hums with clarity and ownership, where every process supports your mission, and where you have the space to focus on what matters most: growing your people and your impact.

That's the power of systems done right. I've seen it transform organizations—like the credit union that cut decision-making time in half and boosted engagement by 25% just by streamlining their workflows.

This isn't about perfection; it's about progress. So, take the next step. Audit your systems, clear the bottlenecks, and build a foundation that doesn't depend on you alone.

You're not just creating a business—you're crafting a legacy of sustainable success that will outlive the chaos and carry your team to new heights. Lead boldly, and watch what happens when your systems scale.

Bringing It All Together

The Build phase is about laying the groundwork for lasting success:

- **Cultivating a thriving culture**: Start with the soil—your people. Shape an environment where trust, purpose, and engagement drive everything.

- **Building proven frameworks**: Implement practical tools like the Big Five—Culture, Service, Growth, Finances, Systems—in the right order to align your team and amplify impact.

- **Creating sustainable momentum**: Design systems, plans, and rhythms that empower your team to scale without you carrying the load.

By doing this, you create a strong foundation, rooted in clarity and purpose, that fuels consistent, scalable growth and sets your team up to win, season after season.

PART THREE: CULTIVATE

KEEPING YOUR TEAM STRONG

IN EVERY SEASON

Chapter 12: The Drift

Why Great Teams Slide and How to Catch It Early

"Success isn't built in one big move. It's sustained in the rhythms that follow."

You've assessed the truth and built a strong foundation.

Now, the Cultivate phase of the ABC Framework begins—the work of sustaining great teams through intentional, repeatable rhythms that protect progress and drive results.

Cultivate isn't about flashy wins or starting over; it's about nurturing what works, refining what doesn't, and ensuring your team thrives, season after season. The greatest threat to this momentum is **Drift**—the slow, silent erosion of clarity, energy, and systems that pulls teams toward stagnation.

Cultivate is the antidote, the daily commitment to tend your organization's soil—its culture, systems, and rhythms—to keep it vibrant. In the chapters ahead, we'll equip you to spot and stop Drift, build accountability without micromanaging, create rhythms that sustain success, and run meetings that spark progress. Let's dive in and make your success last.

The battle against Drift starts with understanding its danger. Drift isn't a sudden crisis; it's the gradual fading of what once worked, triggered by distraction or complacency.

According to Harvard Business Review, over 70% of change initiatives fail, not from poor planning, but from inconsistent follow-through. When leaders stop showing up with intention, meetings lose purpose, scorecards turn into checklists, and your best people disengage, sensing the absence of the vision that once fueled them.

The result is frustration, flattened results, and a culture that withers. In this chapter, we'll uncover how to spot Drift early and stop it with deliberate cultivation, keeping your team's clarity and energy alive.

Drift Happens Slowly

Imagine you're a gardener who plants a vibrant garden in the spring. You've done the hard work—prepping the soil, planting seeds, setting up trellises.

But then summer hits, and you get busy. You skip watering for a few days, overlook the weeds, and forget to fertilize.

Slowly, those plants droop. Some die. Your systems are no different.

When meetings aren't revisited, they turn stale. When scorecards shift from conversation starters to mindless checklists, they lose impact. When rhythms go unattended, Drift sets in.

And your best people? They feel it most—they disengage because the clarity and purpose they once thrived on have faded. Cultivation stops this slide. It's the daily commitment to tend, prune, and nurture, ensuring your team's garden doesn't just survive but flourishes.

The Antidote to Drift: Reinvesting in What Works

Drift sneaks in quietly, eroding the clarity and energy that fuel great teams. It's not a loud crisis—it's the slow fade of systems and purpose when we stop paying attention.

Common Signs of Drift

When Drift creeps in, it shows up in subtle ways. Watch for these red flags—they're your signal to reinvest in the basics:

- Check-ins are skipped or feel like going through the motions.

- Scorecards are filled out but gather dust, never driving action.

- Core values fade from conversations, becoming wall art instead of guiding principles.

- Your best people start disengaging quietly, pulling back their energy or ideas.

These signs don't scream for attention, but they're loud enough if you're listening. The good news? You can stop Drift before it takes hold. The antidote lies in doubling down on what works—deliberate, consistent rhythms that keep your team aligned and thriving.

The solution is simple, though not always easy: a leader who keeps reinvesting in proven frameworks. Specifically, it's about leaning into the *Accountability Rhythm Framework*, the *Success Loop*, and the *Winning Meeting Format* (all detailed in the following chapters). These aren't just tools—they're the heartbeat of sustainable growth. They create a culture of accountability, focus, and momentum that protects your team from slipping into stagnation.

As the leader, you set the tone. If you chase shiny new trends or drop initiatives when they lose their sparkle, your team will mirror that inconsistency. They'll lose trust in the direction you're setting. But if you stay steady—committing to these rhythms even when it's not glamorous—your team will stay steady with you. Consistency builds something powerful: a culture where accountability and growth aren't just ideas but the way you operate. Reinvest in these rhythms, and you'll not only stop Drift but turn it into momentum that carries your team forward, season after season.

Chapter 13: Rhythm > Hype
Accountability in Action

You prevent drift before it starts by building **active accountability,** without micromanaging. This is where a lot of leaders get stuck. They either micromanage because they don't trust the process, or they check out and hope the system will run itself.

Neither approach works. And over time, both lead to the same outcome: drift.

With active accountability, you create a system that keeps your team focused, responsible, and aligned, without you needing to babysit every task.

You already have the tools. Back in the Build phase, you created the structure, scorecards, development plans, and role clarity. Now, in Cultivate, it's time to bring those tools to life.

Why Accountability Falls Apart

Most accountability issues aren't because someone isn't doing their job. They're because the expectations aren't clear, the follow-up isn't consistent, or the system fades over time.

I've seen this happen in organizations of every size. A team launches new systems, they start strong, and for a few weeks everything is running smoothly. But then someone skips a one-on-one. A scorecard doesn't get updated. A deadline moves without a real reason.

Before long, no one's holding the line, and the team begins to drift.

That's why accountability has to be designed into your rhythm.

What Real Accountability Looks Like

Real accountability is visible. Measurable. Structured.

You lead the system that manages the work. When done right, it creates clarity, trust, and a culture where performance thrives.

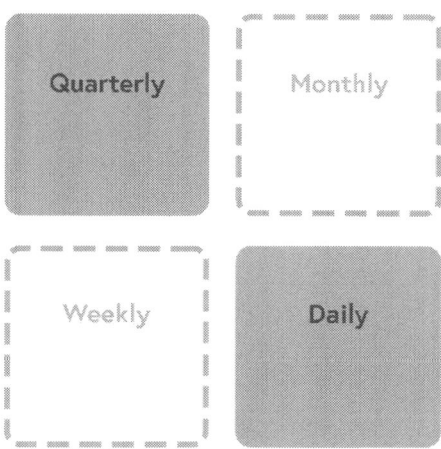

That's where the **Accountability Rhythm Framework** comes in. This model breaks your leadership cadence into four simple layers, Quarterly,

Monthly, Weekly, and Daily, to keep your team aligned from high-level strategy all the way down to micro-moments.

Quarterly Rhythm - Strategy | Reflection | Alignment

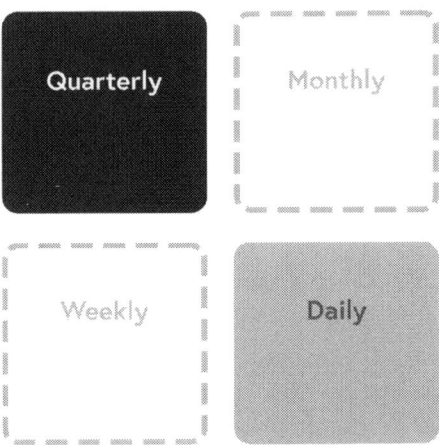

The Quarterly Commitment: A Leader's Role in Cultivation

I recommend every leader schedule one consistent practice that prevents drift before it starts: the Quarterly Commitment.

Every 90 days, you must set aside time to assess what's working, what's not, and where your systems need tuning.

Consistency is key. Treat this quarterly rhythm just like your financials or board reports. It's part of how you lead the business.

One client in Upstate NY embraced this fully. For 18 months, they've committed to quarterly reviews, development plan refreshes, and regular leadership check-ins.

The results? Turnover dropped to zero. Growth has remained in the 25% range for over a year. Culture is so strong they're expanding into a larger building. Their systems didn't drift, they matured.

Why? Because the leader made cultivation a non-negotiable.

You realign the team around the goals, culture, and systems that matter most. It sharpens focus and clears the clutter.

Key practices to revisit each quarter:

- **Culture & engagement pulse surveys** – Check the temperature of your team.

- **Strengths assessments** – Are people playing to their strengths?

- **Scorecard effectiveness** – Are you measuring what matters?

- **Development plan updates** – What growth has happened, and what's next?

- **Success Loop review** – Is your rhythm creating results?

Treat this like a tune-up for your team. Create space for reflection, not just reporting.

Monthly Rhythm - Coaching | Planning | Correction

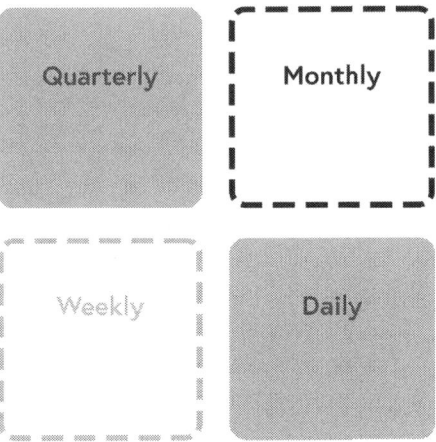

This is where you move from strategy to structure. Monthly rhythms help people *grow* and *stay on track*.

Use this time to:

- Hold structured 1:1 coaching sessions

- Track growth progress and project milestones

- Celebrate KPI progress and recognize wins

- Review bench strength and leadership readiness

- Detect early signs of drift before they grow into bigger issues

Don't wait for annual reviews to give people feedback. Monthly conversations drive real development.

Weekly Rhythm - Execution | Ownership | Momentum

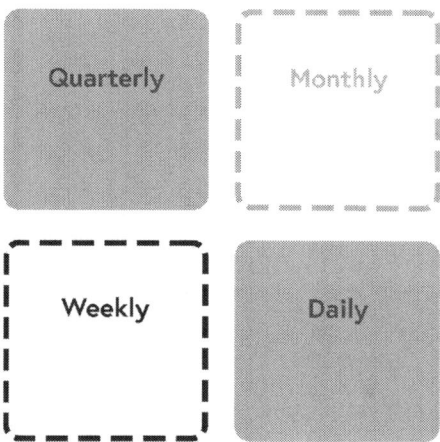

Weekly rhythms are where accountability becomes visible. It's your chance to reinforce clarity, share wins, and address friction early, before it builds up.

Use your **Winning Meeting Format** (I'll teach this in a couple chapters) to structure your weekly team meetings. Track scorecards, discuss ownership, and reset expectations when needed.

Your weekly rhythm should answer these questions:

- What did we accomplish?

- What got in the way?

- Who owns what next?

- How do we win this week?

Meetings are where culture either compounds or collapses. Stick to the format. Protect the rhythm.

Daily Rhythm - Connection | Visibility | Micro-Alignment

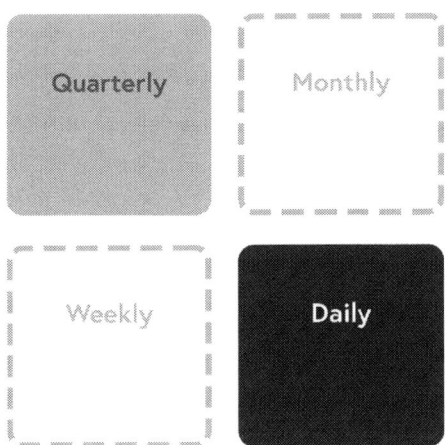

Daily rhythms don't need to be formal. But they do need to be intentional.

Touch points like morning huddles, a quick Slack check-in, or a 10-minute debrief can keep your team aligned and energized. It's also a chance to celebrate micro-wins, provide real-time feedback, and show that you're present and paying attention.

You're managing the energy, clarity, and connection of your team.

A quick "What's your top priority today?" question in a group chat goes a long way.

Why Structure Builds Trust

Some leaders hesitate to add more structure, worried it will feel rigid or controlling. But in my experience, structure is what builds freedom.

When people know the expectations, have the tools, and trust the rhythm, they show up more confident, more focused, and more engaged.

One client I worked with implemented this rhythm across their leadership team. Within 6 months, turnover dropped by 40% because they held their people more accountable.

They stopped letting expectations slide. They gave regular feedback. They coached early and often. And the team responded with buy-in, energy, and performance.

You don't need to manage every detail, but you do need to **manage the system** that manages the details.

How to Start Building Your Rhythm

You don't have to overhaul everything all at once. Start small and build.

Here's one way to ease into this rhythm:

1. **Pick one layer to strengthen** (Monthly one on one's are a great place to start).

2. **Document a simple checklist** for each meeting or touchpoint.

3. **Ask your team for feedback.** What's working? What's not?

4. **Protect the rhythm**. Even when things get busy.

Rhythm builds trust. Trust fuels performance. And performance, over time, becomes your culture.

Chapter 14: The Success Loop
Building Cycles of Motivation That Stick

Maintaining momentum is key. Without it, progress can slow, morale can dip, and achieving long-term success can feel like an uphill battle.

This is where the **Success Loop** comes into play. Think of it as a continuous cycle that keeps motivation high, progress on track, and team morale strong. The Success Loop consists of 3 core components: **Motivate**, **Track**, and **Celebrate**.

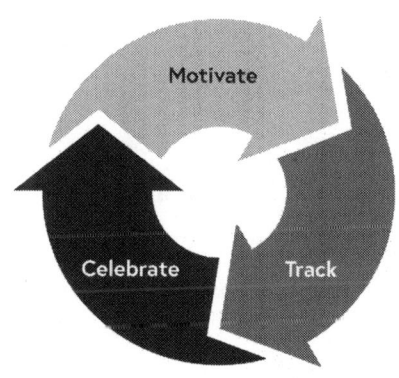

When executed properly, this loop not only boosts engagement but also ensures that goals are constantly being pursued.

Let's break down how each element of the Success Loop can help keep your team focused, motivated, and consistently driving toward results.

Motivate: Keeping the Team Engaged and Inspired

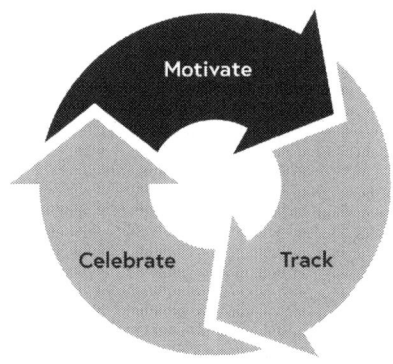

Motivation drives engagement, and **engaged employees are 17% more productive** (Source: Gallup). It's essential to regularly check in on your team's level of motivation to ensure they're inspired to do their best work.

Motivation creates a work environment where people feel valued, recognized, and connected to the bigger picture. People want to know that their work matters, and that their contributions are making a meaningful impact.

That's why it's critical to find 2 to 3 motivators for each team member.

- What makes them tick?

- What work do they enjoy doing?

- Why do they enjoy doing it?

- What motivates them in the work they do?

- Is it to make their family proud? To grow in their career? To maximize their earning potential?

Many areas can motivate our teams, above and beyond our corporate goals. Our job is to find out what motivates them the most through observations, one-on-ones, and their development plans. Use the Development Plans from the Build phase to help guide these conversations. They're not just performance tools, they're motivational tools.

One way to boost motivation is to regularly communicate the vision and mission of the organization and how each person plays a critical role. Whether through team meetings, newsletters, or one-on-one check-ins, **keep the lines of communication open** and remind your team of the greater mission. This sense of purpose is a powerful driver of engagement and motivation.

Track: Monitor Progress to Ensure Goals Are Being Met

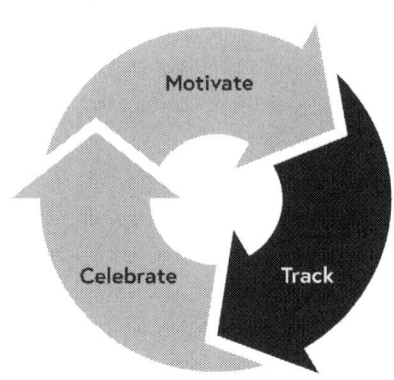

Without clear visibility into how they're performing, team members may feel directionless or uncertain. Tracking provides the clarity they need to stay focused and on track.

Tracking progress examines broader objectives and determines whether you're moving closer to your goals. Studies show that **employees who regularly receive feedback on their performance are 3.6 times more likely to be engaged** than those who don't (Source: Gallup).

This ties back into our look at the Game of Work, referenced back in our Growth pillar under the Build phase. We touched on the importance of having a physical scoreboard, something teams can view daily to track their progress and see where they're at.

One of my clients used this framework to help them track their newest initiative. They wanted to see an increase in sales and struggled to get everyone on board and bought in. After installing this framework and tracking their progress, they increased their sales over the course of 3 weeks by 300%, all by simply having their team track their efforts and focusing on it daily!

Tracking doesn't have to be time-consuming, but it needs to be consistent. You can use your KPIs or progress reports to track individual and team-wide goals. This constant flow of data and feedback helps maintain direction and ensures that teams are continuously working toward their desired results.

Celebrate: Acknowledge Achievements to Reinforce the Right Behaviors and Outcomes

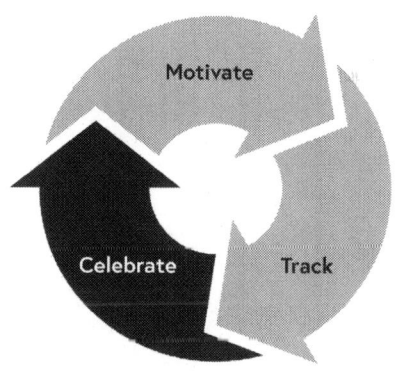

Celebrating accomplishments reinforces positive behavior and outcomes, boosts morale, and strengthens commitment to the organization's goals.

When employees feel their efforts are recognized, they're more likely to repeat those behaviors in the future. **83% of employees who feel recognized are motivated to work harder** (Source: Gallup). People crave acknowledgement, and celebrating achievements fosters a positive and engaged work environment.

Ways to Celebrate Success:

- **Public Recognition**: Praise team members in front of the group, whether in meetings or through internal communications. Public recognition makes people feel valued and boosts morale. One client created a "Kudos Wall" where team members post praise notes about each other. Another ends Friday meetings with "High Five Friday," where each person calls out a team win.

- **Small Wins**: Celebrate small victories along the way, not just the big milestones. Recognizing small successes ensures that momentum keeps building, and the team stays engaged.

- **Reward Systems**: Rewards don't always have to be financial. Offering flexible work hours, additional time off, or team outings can also be effective ways to show appreciation.

Integrating the Success Loop into Your Rhythms

To make the Success Loop a lasting part of your team's culture, weave it into your existing rhythms. Like watering a garden, the loop thrives on consistency, not one-off efforts. Here's how to embed it:

- **Tie to One-on-Ones**: Use regular check-ins to motivate by discussing individual goals and personal drivers, track progress against development plans, and celebrate small wins with personalized praise.

- **Incorporate into Meetings**: Start team meetings with a quick motivator (e.g., a story tying their work to the mission), review scoreboards to track KPIs, and end with recognition, like a "High Five Friday" shout-out.

- **Leverage Quarterly Reviews**: Align the loop with strategic plan reviews. Motivate by revisiting the vision, track progress on quarterly action steps, and celebrate milestones to keep momentum.

- **Use Visual Tools**: Keep a physical or digital Success Loop board in a shared space, updated weekly with motivational quotes, progress metrics, and recent celebrations to reinforce the cycle daily.

By embedding the Success Loop into these rhythms, you ensure it's not just a concept but a living practice that sustains engagement and drives results.

A Continuous Cycle for Lasting Success

The power of the Success Loop is that it never ends, it feeds itself. Motivate, track, celebrate... then do it again. Each time through the cycle, your team builds more clarity, more momentum, and more buy-in.

And because it's ongoing, it protects you from the drop-off that plagues so many organizations once the initial hype fades. Without a rhythm like this in place, motivation slips. Progress stalls. And systems slowly fade into the background.

But when you lead your team through this loop, consistently, they stay engaged. They stay aligned. They stay growing.

This is how you build teams that thrive over the long haul.

Chapter 15: The Winning Meeting Collaboration That Actually Moves the Needle

Meetings are where culture either compounds or collapses.

Too many leaders waste hours in meetings that feel unclear, unproductive, or disconnected from real outcomes. But when used with intention, meetings become a powerful force. They reinforce values, align execution, and build momentum.

That's where the **Winning Meeting Format** comes in. This weekly rhythm advances your culture, accelerating team growth, and keeping everyone clear on what matters most.

The Winning Meeting Format:

Use this simple structure every week to align your team and move the needle:

- **Celebrate** – Acknowledge wins, big or small

- **Ideate** – Create space for creative input

- **Investigate** – Tackle barriers as a team

- **Delegate** – Assign action items clearly

- **Set Goals** – Define what winning looks like this week

This format:

- Reduces wasted time

- Reinforces accountability

- Builds ownership and trust

Teams that follow this structure report **25–30% higher performance and energy retention**. Let's break down how each step builds clarity, drives results, and turns meetings into momentum.

Celebrate – Start With Wins

Starting your meeting with celebration sets the tone for everything that follows. It grounds your team in gratitude, builds momentum, and reinforces a culture of recognition.

Whether it's progress on a big project, a small personal win, or someone going the extra mile, taking a moment to celebrate sends a powerful message: your work matters.

Why it matters: Employees who feel recognized are **2.7x more likely to be engaged** in their work (Gallup).

How to Celebrate in Your Meetings:

- Highlight team or individual achievements

- Call out recent milestones, breakthroughs, or progress

- Encourage peer-to-peer recognition

- Thank someone specifically for something they contributed

This part of the meeting doesn't have to take long, but it does need to be consistent. It builds the emotional lift that fuels the rest of the meeting.

Ideate – Make Space for New Thinking

Innovation happens when we create space for fresh ideas.

The second step, Ideate, is your team's chance to collaborate, explore new possibilities, and think creatively. Whether it's refining a current process or brainstorming a future initiative, this is the time to get the ideas flowing.

Organizations that prioritize innovation are **3x more likely** to experience strong growth (McKinsey).

Tips to Spark Ideation:

- Create a no-judgment zone for ideas, quantity first, quality later

- Ask open-ended questions: "What's a better way to handle ___?"

- Use simple brainstorming tools like sticky notes, whiteboards, or tools like Miro

Over time, this rhythm helps build a culture of improvement. And when innovation becomes a team habit, your organization becomes more adaptive and resilient.

Investigate — Tackle Barriers Head-On

In this phase, you investigate what's not working, and work together to solve it. This isn't about venting. It's about creating solutions that remove friction and accelerate performance.

Teams that collaborate effectively are **5x more likely** to be high-performing (McKinsey).

How to Investigate Effectively:

- Start with real data and examples, avoid vague complaints

- Break down big problems into bite-sized next steps

- Shift from "What's wrong?" to "What can we do about it?"

This step prevents slow decline. Left unaddressed, barriers pile up and become culture killers. Regularly investigating challenges keeps your team agile, aware, and accountable.

Delegate — Assign Action and Ownership

Delegation is where your meeting moves from discussion to execution. It's how clarity turns into action, and how team members know what's expected next.

Organizations with strong delegation practices see **25% higher productivity** (Harvard Business Review).

Tips for Delegation That Sticks:

- Be specific: who is doing what, by when, and what success looks like

- Assign based on strengths and experience

- Track it: follow up on action items from the previous week

Remember, delegation isn't dumping. It's a leadership skill that empowers your team and multiplies momentum.

Set Goals – Define What Winning Looks Like

The final step is to set goals for the week ahead so meetings don't lose forward motion.

Clear, actionable goals create alignment. They give every team member a target to move toward and reinforce that their work connects to something bigger.

Teams that set clear goals are **90% more likely** to hit them (Harvard Business Review).

Best Practices for Goal-Setting:

- Use SMART goals (Specific, Measurable, Achievable, Relevant,

Time-bound)

- Align weekly goals to quarterly outcomes and team KPIs

- Keep it simple, 1 to 3 clear goals per person

When your team leaves with clarity, they move faster and work with more focus. No more vague takeaways or "what now?" moments.

There are going to be setbacks. Curveballs. People will leave unexpectedly. Plans will shift. Growth will bring strain. You'll feel stuck, overwhelmed, or like you're suddenly back at square one.

This is the part most leadership books skip over, but your ability to stay consistent when it gets messy is what separates great leaders from good ones.

Nothing grows without friction.

Even the healthiest teams will experience resistance. Even the best systems will stretch under pressure. And even the most disciplined leaders will face days where everything feels off.

This is where most organizations fall into one of two traps:

- They scrap the system and start over.

- They ignore the problems and hope it'll sort itself out.

Neither option works.

Instead, you need a leadership rhythm that can flex without fracturing, a system strong enough to hold under pressure, and light enough to adapt when the unexpected shows up.

What to Do When Things Go Sideways

Challenges are inevitable: market shifts, team turnover, or unexpected crises can shake even the strongest teams. The Cultivate mindset is about leading through the mess, not dodging it, by reinforcing what works and adapting without losing your foundation.

Like a gardener tending a storm-battered garden, you don't rip out the roots; you stake the plants, clear the debris, and keep nurturing the soil. Here's how to anchor your team when things get tough, overcome common leadership pitfalls, and emerge stronger.

Practical Moves to Stay Anchored

1. **Don't Cancel Your One-on-Ones**: Tough times demand connection. Keep those check-ins to provide clarity, encouragement, and a space for your team to process challenges. Skipping them risks disengagement.

2. **Reconnect to the Mission**: Remind your team why their work matters. Share a story in a meeting or a one-on-one that ties their efforts to the bigger picture, reigniting purpose.

3. **Adjust Without Restarting**: Don't overhaul your systems

when things break. Tweak what's in place—maybe lighten the scorecard or simplify a meeting agenda—to maintain rhythm without starting from scratch.

Overcoming Common Leadership Challenges

Leading through chaos often trips up even seasoned leaders. Here are three common pitfalls and how to navigate them:

- **Distractions**: Chasing shiny new solutions instead of reinforcing existing systems. *Fix*: Lead by example, sticking to your rhythms (like weekly scorecard reviews) to show they matter, even in a storm.

- **Inconsistency**: Dropping systems after a few weeks when results aren't immediate. *Fix*: Commit to consistency, especially when it's inconvenient. Harvard Business Review notes that 70% of employees adopt company values more deeply when leaders model behavior consistently.

- **Resistance**: Team pushback on rhythms that feel "new" or "extra." *Fix*: Invite feedback openly in one-on-ones or meetings to address concerns and build buy-in.

Three Questions to Anchor You in the Mess

When everything feels up in the air, pause and ask:

1. What's one rhythm we can hold onto this week (e.g., a quick team

huddle or scorecard check)?

2. Who on the team needs extra clarity or encouragement right now?

3. What needs to flex (e.g., a lighter meeting cadence) without being forgotten?

These questions keep you grounded, ensuring you lead with stability, not stress.

Rhythms That Work

To sustain the Cultivate mindset, lean on these proven rhythms:

- **Quarterly Check-Ins**: Realign systems and adjust goals to stay on track.

- **Monthly Coaching**: Track development and encourage growth through one-on-ones.

- **Weekly Scorecard Reviews**: Keep goals visible and progress clear.

- **Daily Touchpoints**: Quick stand-ups or messages to reinforce energy and alignment.

One client, after navigating a messy season, summed it up perfectly: "I used to rebuild everything when things broke. Now I tweak the system we have."

That's the Cultivate mindset—don't reinvent, reinforce. Protect your soil, make grounded decisions, and stick to your rhythms, even when the sky feels stormy. Consistency compounds, building teams that don't just survive tough seasons but thrive through them, season after season.

Great Teams Don't Happen By Accident

Teams are built, nurtured, and sustained through intentional leadership. And the best leaders don't rely on gut instinct or hope, they follow a system. You've already explored each phase of the ABC Framework:

- **Assess**, where clarity begins.

- **Build**, where structure takes shape.

- **Cultivate**, where consistency delivers results.

Each phase is powerful on its own. But when practiced together, in rhythm, they create what I call **leadership momentum**, a flywheel that picks up speed with every cycle. When you lead with the full ABC cycle, your organization becomes predictably excellent. Here's what starts to happen:

Your team gets aligned, not just on goals, but on values, priorities, and roles.

This alignment isn't theoretical, it transforms organizations.

Consider **One Detroit Credit Union**, which faced leadership transitions that could have destabilized their progress. By leaning into the Build phase's succession planning, they crafted a clear roadmap to identify and develop future leaders.

The result? A 35% increase in leadership retention over three years and a surge in team member engagement. Korn Ferry's research supports this: organizations with robust succession plans are 33% more likely to maintain leadership effectiveness. One Detroit's commitment to intentional systems ensured stability and growth, even in uncertainty.

But alignment is just the start. The ABC Framework also builds lasting momentum through strategic vision and execution.

Momentum builds because you're not restarting every quarter, you're reinforcing and expanding what works.

This momentum can redefine a business's future, as seen with **Greybeard Steel**, a custom steel company at a crossroads as its owners planned retirement.

Using the full ABC Framework, they didn't just plan a transition, they shaped a legacy.

We honed their culture, hired for growth, and developed a team member into a General Manager over two years, backed by a strategic ownership plan. Today, they enjoy double-digit profits, record customers, and a team driving sustainable growth, with the owners advising from retirement.

Their story shows how Assess, Build, and Cultivate create a flywheel of success that carries a business forward, even through major shifts.

This kind of momentum fuels engagement, as teams see their efforts translate into tangible impact.

Engagement rises because people understand how they fit into the big picture, and they feel valued for it.

That's exactly what happened at **State CS Employees Federal Credit Union**, where a focus on team development through the Build and Cultivate phases transformed their culture. By regularly revisiting strengths assessments and development plans in one-on-ones, they fostered an environment of continuous growth.

The outcome? A 25% improvement in team performance within a year and a 29% drop in turnover, aligning with Gallup's finding that organizations investing in development see a 21% productivity boost. State CS's story proves that nurturing people within a system creates ownership and impact that lasts.

Leadership capacity grows as systems, scorecards, and rhythms take pressure off the few and activate the many.

What Happens When It's Incomplete

If you're only Assessing, you may know the problems, but you'll struggle to fix them. If you're Building without Assessing, you risk building systems that miss the mark. If you're Cultivating without structure, you're spinning plates with no plan. But when you lead through each phase - Assess, Build, Cultivate - you create a cycle that's self-reinforcing.

Issues get spotted early. Plans are built on truth. Wins are sustained through rhythm and accountability. And your team feels it.

So, commit to the ABC Framework with intention and watch your team soar. You've got the tools, the stories, and the system to transform your organization into one that's aligned, engaged, and unstoppable.

Embrace the rhythm, stay steady, and lead boldly - you've got this!

Thank you for investing your time with me in these pages; now go build a team that wins, season after season.

Your Next Step

You've just uncovered the ABC Framework, a proven system to Assess your team's truth, Build a foundation for growth, and Cultivate rhythms that sustain success.

Every page of *Catalyst* has equipped you with tools to transform your team, step by intentional step. Apply it consistently, and you'll see progress.

But here's the truth I've learned from guiding hundreds of leaders: *the right partnership doesn't just move you forward, it propels you.*

Imagine you're leading a team stuck in reactive mode, battling disengagement or stalled momentum.

You *could* grind through, applying the ABC Framework on your own, like driving a winding road from San Francisco to Denver. You'll get there, but it'll take time, energy, and trial-and-error.

Now imagine boarding a jet with a seasoned pilot who knows the route, anticipates turbulence, and lands you at your destination faster, with clarity and confidence. That's the power of a guided partnership.

This book is your roadmap, but for leaders ready to collapse time and amplify results, I offer a hands-on, customized coaching process.

It's not about handing you a playbook—it's about walking alongside you to apply the ABC Framework directly to your business, aligning your team, and building a culture of trust, execution, and unstoppable momentum. This isn't for everyone. It's for:

- **Mission-driven leaders** who refuse to settle for average.

- **Teams committed to transformation**, ready to uplevel from the top down.

- **Organizations craving clarity**, eager to replace chaos with rhythm and results.

I've seen this process work wonders. Credit unions have boosted engagement by 25% through targeted development plans. Businesses have doubled profits by embedding strategic rhythms. Leaders have found peace of mind, knowing their legacy is secure. These aren't just outcomes—they're proof that the ABC Framework, paired with the right guidance, creates predictable excellence.

If you're ready to fly—faster, bolder, and with less strain—let's talk.

Scan the QR code below to access a short form. It'll help us both determine if working together would be the right fit.

From there, we'll schedule a focused conversation to explore your goals and map out how this process can accelerate your success.

You have the framework. You have the vision.

The only question is: *How fast do you want to soar?*

Take the leap. Let's build a team that wins, season after season.

Scan the QR Code Now and Start Your Journey

Acknowledgements

There's no such thing as a solo success. This book, and the work behind it, was only possible because of the people who've stood beside me, encouraged me, and challenged me to keep going.

First, thank you Jesus for loving and setting me free. You bring meaning to everything, including this book.

To my beautiful wife Kelly, thank you for your love, patience, and unwavering belief in me. And to Oliver, Henry, Elliot, and Mykah, who remind me every day why this work matters and what legacy really looks like.

You are my greatest joy.

To Jonathan Heston, your wisdom, feedback, and ability to sharpen the message have made a huge difference. I'm grateful for your voice in this process, in my business, and for your friendship through it all.

To my assistant Faith. Your work has helped us serve our clients even better and your help launching this book has been amazing.

To my editor Fred Aceves and designer Sarah Gephart. Your contributions to this book and eye for detail took this book to a whole new level.

To my clients, this book is really for you. You've taken the frameworks, lived them out, and made them better through your courage, your questions, and your commitment to growth. You've trusted me to walk with you through the messy middle, through the wins and the setbacks. You've helped refine this process into something real, something practical, something that works.

Thank you for inspiring me. For pushing this work further. For letting me be part of your story.

This book may have my name on the cover, but it's been shaped by all of you.

Lead Boldly,

Michael

Made in the USA
Columbia, SC
15 May 2025

57977009R00104